THE RIDDLE OF GRACE

The Riddle of Grace

Applying Grace to the Christian Life

Scott Hoezee

WILLIAM B. EERDMANS PUBLISHING COMPANY
GRAND RAPIDS, MICHIGAN / CAMBRIDGE, U.K.

© 1996 Wm. B. Eerdmans Publishing Co.
255 Jefferson Ave. S.E., Grand Rapids, Michigan 49503 /
P. O. Box 163, Cambridge CB3 9PU U.K.

Printed in the United States of America

01 00 99 98 97 96   7 6 5 4 3 2 1

Library of Congress Cataloging-in-Publication Data

Hoezee, Scott, 1964-
The riddle of grace: applying grace to the Christian life /
Scott Hoezee.
p.   cm.
Includes bibliographical references.
ISBN 0-8028-4129-5 (alk. paper)
1. Grace (Theology)   I. Title.
BT761.2.H58 1995
234 — dc20   95-45170
                                                  CIP

For Rosemary,
my love, my companion,
my confidant, my best friend,
now and always

Contents

Acknowledgments

I AM SO VERY grateful to a number of people who helped make this book a reality. First of all, I thank Neal Plantinga, who, in the nine years I have known him as professor, mentor, and friend, has shaped me in more ways than I am aware. He was also the first to read this entire manuscript, he offered exceedingly helpful advice, and, as usual, he gave me a great boost of encouragement. For that, and more, I give him my thanks.

I also thank four others who took the time to read and offer comment on the manuscript: Susanne Jordan, Jack Roeda, Jim Vanden Bosch, and Clarence Vos. Each brought a unique perspective and expertise to this work and, while any deficiencies in the final product are my own, a number of its better points came from them. I also gratefully acknowledge the two congregations I have served: Second Christian Reformed Church in Fremont, Michigan, and Calvin Christian Reformed Church in Grand Rapids. Each heard sermons during the last five years that contained bits and pieces of this book and each, in one way or another, also contributed to my thinking in this area by offering helpful feedback as well as ample time for study and reflection.

I also thank Sandra De Groot of Eerdmans for wanting to see the completed manuscript and for helping make sure that it saw the light of day. I thank my dear parents, Edward and Virginia, who raised me in grace by making sure that my brother Tim and I always knew that our acceptance in their sight was by the love of grace and that the same would also always hold true with God. And lastly I thank my wife

Rosemary, who believed in this project from the beginning, who encouraged me all along the way, and whose joy at the news of its publication equalled my own — to her I owe something more than mere gratitude for being such a lovely, gracious, and grace-giving presence in my life every day.

SCOTT HOEZEE

For it is by grace you have been saved, through faith — and this not from yourselves, it is the gift of God.

— Ephesians 2:8

There are few words so strange to most of us than "sin" and "grace." They are strange, just because they are so well known.

— Paul Tillich

Introduction

THE 1990 PBS documentary "*Amazing Grace* with Bill Moyers" amply highlights the profound impact this famous hymn has had since its composition two centuries ago. Through interviews with celebrities, choir directors, and ordinary churchgoing folk from all over the country, Moyers shows viewers that the lyrics of ex–slave trader John Newton continue to move, touch, and inspire people many years after their composition. But most of the people interviewed in the film testified that even more than the hymn proper, it is the grace of which the hymn speaks that resonates in their souls, touching their personal experience on a level that nearly defies description.

The film illustrates the power of this grace through several poignant vignettes in which grace transforms situations that would otherwise be filled with hopelessness, sorrow, and despair. One segment gives "Amazing Grace" new punch as the viewer witnesses a choir of life-sentence inmates talking and then singing about the grace that has saved convicted "wretches" like themselves. In another segment, the Harlem Boys' Choir nicely displays the hope of grace as it reaches inner-city children who live in a burned-over world of shattered dreams and dead-end streets. When their young voices blend to croon those old familiar words, only the coldest of hearts could fail to be moved by the transforming power and deep hope that shines like a beacon in the otherwise dark alleys of their world.

But while it is easy to view this film through the religious lens of Christianity, a more objective viewing reveals that the "grace" so

1

eloquently celebrated in the film is mostly generic. Although the Christian idea of grace through Jesus Christ is the subtext underlying the words of several interviewees, it is seldom made explicit. A number of the celebrities interviewed seemed to regard grace as a kind of universal entity or force that one could discover or encounter during periods of crisis or hurt — a power for strengthening the weak and shoring up the wobbly. Singer Judy Collins, whose 1970 rendition of "Amazing Grace" yielded a Top 20 hit, claimed that, for her, grace is a kind of "inner experience of another dimension" from which she draws solace and peace. She feels that this was why so many of the cultural dropouts of the 1960s were drawn to the hymn — it gave them a connection to some other realm at a time when the present realm was in turmoil and confusion.

Others in the film likewise appeared to regard grace as something that could be "found" and that, once so discovered, could help see one through the "many dangers, toils, and snares" of life. A few even expressed what bordered on a psychological view of the hymn, claiming that this cosmos-permeating "grace" was something that could help one build self-esteem instead of always feeling wretched. Strikingly, the name "Jesus" was nearly wholly absent from the testimonies of those interviewed. (But then, except for a reference to "The Lord" in verse 3, John Newton's original hymn also does not mention "Jesus" or "God," thus making it ripe for others to pour generic content into its words.)

But of course this film was not about religious grace per se but about the power of a famous *hymn*. Taken on its own level, this is surely one of the best television documentaries of the past ten years. Many who watched it found themselves humming the tune for days after, happily being uplifted by its melody and message. But I point out the generic, misunderstood grace of some of those interviewed in the film in order to introduce a broader theme: Exactly what is the "amazing grace" of which we sing and on which we Christians have staked our lives? Do we understand its full implications, or has its specific power in Christ been drained of meaning for us, even as it appears to have been for some of those in the film?

Of course Christians are unlikely to regard God's grace in anything other than a purely religious, biblical light. But the question persists: Do we know what it means to be a graced people? In the pages ahead

I hope to think constructively about this vital question as it applies to some concrete situations in the church and in culture.

I am painfully aware that the subject of grace is frequently written on and that this book could therefore be buried in a heap of other "grace books." But I earnestly hope to break new ground, to cover territory previously unexplored by other writers on this subject. It appears that many of the books written on grace today focus on the *sustaining* power of grace in the various difficulties of life. These books are promoted as great sources of comfort, as helping readers "really feel and live" the power of God's grace. Some such books could lead one to believe that the main obstacle to living a life of grace is just not feeling good enough about yourself. In a grimly ironic twist, some contemporary treatments of grace go so far in this direction that they could almost be included in the "self-help" genre currently so popular in some segments of Christian publishing (and one wonders what Saint Paul would make of "self-help grace"!).

But maybe this is not so surprising given other trends in American Christianity, especially the recent downplaying of sin. In his book *Not the Way It's Supposed to Be* (Grand Rapids: Eerdmans, 1995), Neal Plantinga notes that one of the main dangers in losing sight of our sin is that it makes grace uninteresting and unnecessary. Indeed, as consciousness of sin has been slipping in recent times, grace has likewise undergone a number of transformations.

Where once grace was seen to be the *only* power that could save woefully wretched sinners, now it is more of a polish to shine up the egos of people who were not so bad off to begin with. Where once grace was life-giving water for people dying of dehydration in sin's desert, now it's more of a cocktail sipped on the veranda of self-esteem — a potable imbibed not so much to save a wretched life as to cop a pleasant buzz in an already good life. Indeed, Martin Marty recently reported that a new Roman Catholic version of "Amazing Grace" has replaced the lyric "that saved a wretch like me" with "that saved and strengthened me." But from what are we saved and for what are we strengthened?

All such approaches to grace gloss over or ignore the kinds of challenges and difficulties that grace introduces and that I plan to highlight in the pages ahead. By that I do not mean to imply that books that bring out grace's comfort and sustaining strength are wholly wrong or unnecessary. For the grace of God *is* a profound comfort. There is tremendous liberating power in the forgiving grace of God, a power that should help believers ultimately overcome feelings of wretchedness, worthlessness, and guilt. Christians do need to see their worth in the light of God's love and grace.

There is also tremendous sustaining strength in God's grace, strength that should empower believers through the many "dangers, toils, and snares" that confront them. Those in the PBS documentary who testified to a sense of "the Other" in their lives, to a sense that there was available to them a power and a grace to lend aid and comfort, were not wrong — not even from a Christian point of view.

But the grace of God is finally more than a mere comfort or source of pleasant strength. In fact, we could define grace as being first of all that power of God, rooted in his abiding love, by which God forgives the sinful, accepts the unacceptable, revives the spiritually dead, and so enables a reunion between the Creator and his wayward creatures. Grace is the power of God's love that crashes (and sometimes creeps) unexpectedly and undeservedly into our lives, thus granting a spiritual restoration we could never have achieved on our own. That we are saved by grace alone, even though we did not deserve it, is certainly the comforting good news of the gospel. But the power of God's grace does not end there.

For as amazingly powerful as grace's ability to forgive our sins is, God's grace actually contains even more energy. Beyond forgiveness, grace also aims to transform our way of life. Encountering God's grace is a formative, creative moment as a result of which a person is not only graced by God's love but also becomes *gracious* because of God's love.

By saying we must be "gracious" I do not mean being kind, deferential, courteous, or polite, which we typically signify when we say, "She certainly is a gracious person." Rather, I mean "gracious" in the sense of being *grace-like*, of showing forth in our own lives some of the qualities of God's grace in Christ.

Being gracious in this sense thus means having the ability to forgive others as we have been forgiven (and to *want* to forgive even when we grapple with its seeming impossibility). Being gracious means having the ability to see worth and value in people beyond what they deserve, despite their unattractive qualities, and irrespective of what they can do for us. Being gracious means having the ability to frame all of life by the grace that has saved us, thus maintaining the proper perspective on sin, morality, and good works, as well as on our relationship with non-Christians. In short, being gracious means living a distinctively Christian life that daily revels in the power of God's grace while also allowing it to inform and thus transform ordinary ways of living.

Although this book aims to remind us again of what it means to be *saved* by grace, we will be even more concerned to explore what it means to *live* graciously as a result of that salvation. As we will see, living a gracious life in imitation of God's grace can become pretty complicated in a society that, in so many ways, does not appreciate or celebrate grace. While grace may be a comfort, living that grace on a daily basis can be a rather nettlesome challenge as it threatens to alter usual ways of thinking, acting, and living. For low self-esteem is surely not the only obstacle to living a gracious life (it may not even be the main obstacle). Even the strength we receive from grace is more complicated than some authors lead us to believe. For it is not strength, as some participants in the documentary conceived of it — namely, power to boost ordinary day-to-day activities. Rather, it is strength that aims to reshape day-to-day activities into something extraordinary!

Thus, one of my aims will be to highlight some typical ways of thinking in order to show how contrary they are to the biblical ideas of grace and graciousness. More than we know, we constantly encounter forces that undermine both our awareness of how we were saved in the first place (by the power of God's grace alone) and our ability to live graciously in imitation of that divine grace. Some of these forces come from outside of us — from society and, unhappily, even from the church. Others come from inside of us — from our own skewed ideas of what is fair or how we reckon value.

What we will discover is that in both the church and in the broader culture, the grace of the gospel and the graciousness it is supposed to engender are often at odds with the status quo. For this reason grace is more complex than some writers, teachers, and preachers admit. In what follows we will tackle some subjects that are so snarled that easy solutions cannot be proffered. Indeed, my intention is not to give definitive words of advice on the subjects here presented, but rather to suggest directions in which we can begin thinking, discussing, and reflecting further on these vital topics. Given the central place of grace in the gospel of Jesus Christ, these subjects surely warrant such further reflection and development.

Chapter One, which probes the Scriptures to discover the biblical underpinnings of the doctrine of grace, is the most technical. Where in the Bible do we learn that grace is the power of God's love? How might such knowledge help us imitate this grace in our lives? Although most of this book is practical, we cannot build the practical unless we first lay the proper biblical, theological foundation. Thus we will first go to the Old Testament to see where we can find hints and whispers of New Testament grace. Then we will turn to the Gospels and the writings of Paul to investigate just what it means to say that we are "saved by grace" and what this implies for the gracious lives that are supposed to follow.

Chapter Two wrestles with a key dimension of the gracious life, namely, living gratefully. Since grace is the greatest gift a person could ever receive, it is only natural to seek ways to say "Thank You" to the God who gave it. But, as we will see, some writers, in trying to celebrate the utterly free, no-strings-attached nature of God's saving grace in Christ, tend for that very reason to downplay the need for a transformed life of gratitude. Robert Farrar Capon is an eloquent writer on the subject of grace, yet he nearly severs the connection between being graced and, in turn, being gracious. We need to explore the tender gospel threads that weave together receiving grace and the resulting distinctive life of the Christian.

On the other side of the spectrum, however, are those who confuse the gracious life of the saved with the grace that brought them there in the first place. Unhappily, it is altogether too easy to regard the fruit of grace as in fact being the root of salvation, such that the point of comparison between the Christian and the non-Christian becomes not "amazing grace" but the morality of the former over against the immorality of the latter. But such a perspective is just as backward as thinking that the peaches on a peach tree brought about the roots under the earth!

The biblical teaching is that the root of salvation is grace alone. It is this grace that nourishes and enables the production of spiritual fruit in the Christian life. Grace comes first; graciousness follows. To confuse the fruit with the root is not only ridiculous; it is also deadly in that it cuts off the Christian from his or her true source of spiritual nourishment.

So what is it, in God's eyes, that distinguishes an upstanding church-goer from a pimp who peddles sex for a price? Is it that the one *is* upstanding and churchgoing and the other is not, or is it finally grace alone? If it is grace alone, where does that leave the lifestyle of the Christian? Why do we need to bother with this whole matter of graciousness? The Reformed tradition has made a great deal of the need to live "the grateful life," but we need to ponder the ways in which we may misconstrue this gratitude and the perils to which it can therefore introduce us.

Chapter Three moves out of a specifically church context into a broader realm: Understanding God's saving grace and then living the gracious life in the "pull-yourself-up-by-your-own-bootstraps" society of capitalism. The New Testament teaches that we cannot earn or achieve our own salvation. It is freely given by God. But what happens to our perspectives on grace when we live in a society of achievers? Might it be that after a while we begin to think that salvation, like everything else we value in our lives, must also be earned or achieved? If we begin to think that way, how likely are we in turn to lead gracious lives? After all, if our being gracious depends on a good imitation of God's saving grace, then watering down God's grace by elevating our own achievements will likewise thin out our Christian distinctiveness.

As we think along these lines, we will also have occasion to ask questions like these: How might Christian businesspeople exercise the best principles of capitalism while at the same time inculcating into themselves and their employees a sense of grace? Or is that itself a wrongheaded question since the realm of business ought not to intersect with the realm of theology? What about those not in business but who still live in a society where most things are reward and punishment but seldom free? If success-oriented capitalism is the air we breathe, are we truly able to understand and live out the implications of the grace that throbs at the heart of our theology? Further, will we communicate grace and graciousness to our children at home and in church, or will they, too, pick up the idea that they must first be good in order to earn God's love?

Chapter Four tackles the touchy matter of church discipline. Nearly all ecclesiastical bodies have some form of discipline for wayward members. But how often do we allow grace to inform even this process? What might it mean to be gracious as God is gracious even in the face of someone's sin — especially if that sin has hurt us personally and deeply? How can we be gracious without appearing to be "soft on sin"?

In general, what distinguishes the church's handling of sin and scandal from that of other institutions in society? When someone is caught in a public sin, what ought our reaction to be? Perhaps when the person does not care and is not penitent, we have some idea of what to do (though, as we will see, even this ought to be more complicated than it often is). But what should be our response when genuine repentance is present? What about ministers caught in scandal? Is automatic dismissal the only possible course of action, or does being gracious lead another way?

Between these chapters I have placed meditations on grace from three well-known Old Testament stories. I have chosen these passages partly to uncover their real meaning as opposed to the cleaned-up Sunday school versions most of us learned as children. As we will see, we can appreciate the real grace of these stories only when we do *not* strip them down and clean them up. But another reason for looking at these Old Testament stories is to recognize that the grace of God is indeed active throughout the whole Bible and not just in the New Testament (a point I also make in Chapter One). For the God of the Bible is a God of grace from first to last.

This book is intended both for those who write sermons and for those who listen to them. I trust that fellow preachers and worship leaders will find it helpful to them in their weekly challenge of serving up a nourishing meal of grace from God's Word. But I also believe that this book will edify all of us as Christians as we struggle to find, and then to incarnate, the meaning of God's grace in our day-to-day activities. Thus I hope that this book contains enough theology to foster further reflection by those who have a formal theological background but is at the same time clear and interesting enough to hold the attention of any thoughtful Christian who wants to explore grace in greater detail.

None of the issues addressed in this book is easy, but each goes to the heart of the church's life in the world. If grace cannot inform and, what is more, *transform* these practices of life into something gracious and lovely, then perhaps God's grace is not so "amazing" after all. Grace is a marvelous power, a transforming power, an all-encompassing power. By it we ought to be comforted, assured, empowered, and enlivened. But as grace seeks to transform our lives, we may also find challenge, discomfort, and a humble sense of human weakness in the presence of divine superpower. As we explore these themes in the pages ahead, my hope is that we will conclude with the only fitting response to God's grace in Christ: Doxology.

CHAPTER ONE

Grace and Scripture

WE CAN FAIRLY SAY that most people come to church to hear about grace. In the comparatively brief time during which I have been preaching, I have had numerous people tell me how much they need a weekly dose of the gospel or good news of God's grace. People ranging from Ph.D.s to those who have failed to graduate from eighth grade, the young as well as the old, deeply thirst to hear over and again the old, old story that, as a friend of mine put it, "is almost too good to be true." Perhaps we hunger for this because of yet another week of being disappointed by our own sinfulness. Perhaps we long to hear about grace simply because we live in a world so shot through with evil that merely watching the network news can cause the sunniest personality to eclipse into depression. But whatever the reason, when Sunday morning comes, most people find themselves more than ready to be reminded that God loves, saves, and accepts them even still.

While nearly all church traditions deliver the cargo of grace each week, the Reformed tradition and its churches have given grace a special prominence. Indeed, anyone raised in a Reformed congregation could scarcely miss the central role grace has played in the life and thought of Reformed theologians from the time of John Calvin onward. As Robert Capon once put it, the Reformers nearly "ranted and raved" about the wonder of grace when they rediscovered it on the pages of Holy Scripture.[1]

1. Robert Farrar Capon, *Between Noon and Three* (San Francisco: Harper and Row, 1982), p. 114.

The "ranting" has continued ever since. Still, despite grace's looming theological significance and despite massive backing from the New Testament letters of Paul, it might surprise many people to discover the comparative absence of "grace" in the four Gospels.

The Greek word most commonly translated "grace" is *charis*, which occurs in one form or another approximately 155 times in the New Testament. But the vast majority of these occurrences are in the writings of Paul. In fact, *charis* occurs only once in the Synoptic Gospels (Luke 2:40) and just three times in the Gospel of John (1:14, 16, 17). Strikingly, the word is wholly absent from the Gospel narratives of Jesus' life (including his preaching and teaching).

What are we to make of such a disparity? In the last two centuries, some critics of the New Testament have alleged that the Jesus with whom most people are acquainted is a distorted Jesus. The apostle Paul, they claim, did not really know much about the historical Jesus, such that the theology constructed by Paul has only tangential connections to the life and teachings of the carpenter from Nazareth. The real historical Jesus, these critics say, is found only in the Gospel traditions, and this Jesus is very different from Paul's version of him.

Does the lack of "grace" in the Gospel narratives lend credence to these theories? If not, we are nonetheless left to ponder the meaning of grace in the Bible. Why *does* it appear so often in New Testament letters but scarcely at all in the Gospels?

Further, what about the Old Testament? One of the earliest heresies of the Christian church came from a teacher named Marcion who claimed, among other things, that the Old Testament God of wrath and law was so different from the New Testament God of love and grace that we must in actuality be dealing with two *different* gods. What about that? Is grace to be found solely in the New Testament (and then mostly in the letters of Paul)? If so, is the central place of grace in Reformed theology perhaps mistaken after all? Is grace a major biblical theme, as we've been claiming these last 400 years, or is its place in Scripture a more modest one?

In this chapter we will try to understand the meaning of grace from both the Old and the New Testaments. After examining some passages where the word "grace" appears, we may be prepared to see why the word receives so little treatment in the Gospels, and yet why the later development of the especially Pauline theological concept is nonetheless wholly warranted *by* the Gospels and, indeed, by the entire Bible.

Before we begin our biblical survey, it should be noted that our focus is a fairly narrow one. Our primary interest throughout this book will be on the power of God's saving grace, not only as it first comes to a person but even more so in its later transformation of that person's life into something "gracious." This may seem merely obvious, but the word "grace" does occasionally carry slightly different nuances.

For instance, "grace" can refer to an ongoing power of endurance during difficult times. When Paul says in 2 Corinthians 8:1, "Now, brothers, we want you to know about the grace that God has given the Macedonian churches,"[2] he refers to a divine power by which those churches were battened down to weather some storms of early church persecution. Likewise in Hebrews 4:16 we are encouraged to pray so that "we might find grace to help us in our time of need." This, too, refers to grace in the sense of God's abiding presence, the staying power of God in the lives of believers. While this strengthening power of God is vital for the Christian life, and while it has ties and affinities to the grace that saves and transforms, it ought also to be distinguished from "grace" as we will mostly refer to it in this book.

In still other places "grace" may refer to a more generic quality of human personality. Luke tells us that Jesus grew up "filled with wisdom, and the grace of God was upon him" (Luke 2:40). This would seem to mean less that he was showing evidences of being saved and more that there was a certain air of piety and wholeness about Jesus. In a more secular setting one can hear similar expressions when people refer to someone as displaying a lot of "personal grace."

Similarly, as we noted in the Introduction, the word "gracious" can be used in a very salvation-specific context ("gracious salvation"), but it can also be used more broadly to refer to a particularly kind or deferential person ("She's very gracious when receiving compliments"). So the words "grace" and "gracious" can be, and frequently are, shorn of a salvation context and are used more generically to describe people's behavior or personality. But when I refer to the Christian's need to be "gracious," I mean someone who knows and celebrates the power of

2. Unless otherwise noted, all Scripture passages will be taken from the New International Version of the Bible.

13

God's grace both in its initial forgiving of his or her sin and in its ongoing operation of shaping that person's perspectives and way of life. To be gracious in this sense is to imitate God's way of relating to us when we also relate to one another.

In a more salvation-specific vein, Paul occasionally uses "grace" to describe the antithesis of "law" or "works." In these uses, then, "grace" is a kind of synecdoche, a "catchall" term. When Paul says, "You who are trying to be justified by law have . . . fallen away from grace" (Gal. 5:4) or ". . . you are not under law, but under grace" (Rom. 6:14b), he is clearly using "grace" as a title for the era of salvation that was introduced decisively through Jesus Christ. While this is a saving grace, most of what I have to say in this book will take a slightly narrower, more personal focus.

But these other usages of "grace" are the exception. By far the bulk of New Testament references to "grace" refer to the gospel core of our being saved in Christ. Grace is how the wrong are righted, how the crooked are made straight, how the guilty are made innocent, how the sooty are made to shine like stars — in short, how the damned are saved. Grace is sin's counter-power in the universe — when grace comes, sin dies.

Grace is so much the counterpunch of sin that the two cannot peacefully coexist. This is why Paul was always flabbergasted to discover those who thought grace was a license to sin all the more (a topic to be taken up in Chapter Two). "Don't you understand?! In grace you died to sin — it's dead, it's gone, it's banished!" Paul ranted. In Paul's view, sinning more so that grace might abound makes no more sense than eating more so that you can lose more weight! Revelling in sin in order to appreciate grace more makes no more sense than trying to appreciate chastity by becoming sexually promiscuous! Willfully to go on sinning because you think God will forgive you anyway makes no more sense than willfully inflicting yourself with tuberculosis because you figure doctors can cure it now anyway.

Grace is sin's mortal foe because grace is first and last the saving power of God. But before we explore the New Testament emphasis on the saving significance of this grace, we need to return to the question put earlier: Is grace a New Testament, Pauline invention? Or does this word (and concept) have such deep roots in the very character of God that we can justifiably claim that it anchors the entire Bible? To answer this, let us begin a study of this word and concept, beginning in the Old Testament.

The Old Testament Witness

At the outset it ought to be freely admitted that the full-blown doctrine of salvation by grace does not gel until the letters of Paul. But lest we fall prey to the heresy of Marcionism, we need to be very clear: The doctrine of God's grace encompasses the entire Bible. But especially in the Old Testament (and in a way also in the Gospels, as we will note further below), the doctrine of grace is like a biblical jigsaw puzzle. That is, the various pieces of the doctrine of salvation by grace were scattered throughout the Bible just waiting for someone like Paul finally to gather them up and fit them together into the big picture. So when, in places like Romans and Galatians, Paul sketches the doctrine of salvation by grace alone, he is not creating something new out of thin air but is merely putting together a picture that existed in the Bible all along, albeit in scattered pieces.

We can begin to locate some of these pieces by looking at the relevant Hebrew vocabulary of the Old Testament. If you searched an English concordance to check on occurrences of the word "grace" in the Old Testament, you might be surprised to find how seldom it appears. In the New International Version of the Old Testament the word "grace" occurs just eight times, several of which have no religious/theological meaning whatsoever (e.g., "a garland to grace your neck").

But of course English concordances are dealing with translations of the original Hebrew. If we are to discover the Old Testament spring for the doctrine of God's grace, we need to plumb deeper to those original Hebrew words that deal with "grace" and "mercy." The Hebrew word most closely associated with the Greek word *charis* ("grace") is *ḥen,* which can mean "grace" but which is more often rendered "favor."[3]

---

3. The Greek translation of the Hebrew Old Testament, the Septuagint, regularly puts the Greek word *charis* in the place of the Hebrew *ḥen.* In general, much of the etymological information in this section was drawn from *Theological Dictionary of the New Testament,* ed. Gerhard Kittel and Gerhard Friedrich (Grand Rapids: Eerdmans, 1974), IX, 372-402.

But this word for "favor" comes from the Hebrew verb *ḥanan,* which means "to show favor." As we will see, the verb form may actually be more important in this study than the noun form.

In general it could be said that *ḥen*/"favor" is less a quality to be found in God and more a quality to be found in the human recipients of God's goodness. In other words, God showered his goodness on those he deemed "favorable" or worthy, as in Genesis 6:8, where we read that "Noah found favor in the eyes of the LORD."

Because such "favor" could incur blessing, a frequently uttered Old Testament prayer says something like, "O God, look on your servant that he might find favor in your sight and so receive your great mercy." (Obviously this is not only dissimilar to the New Testament idea of "grace"; it is very nearly inimical to the idea that we need God's grace precisely because we are *not* favorable in God's eyes because of our sin! This, however, does not indicate a cleft between the theology of the Old Testament and the New, but only that we have here a dissimilarity in some of the relevant vocabulary.)

This kind of "favor" was also frequently sought from other people, such that the line "If I have found favor in your eyes . . ." became a standard prologue to making a request. For instance, someone might say, "If I have found favor in your eyes, please allow me to stay in your house for a while." So although the idea of gaining *God's* grace (where grace is a trait within God) is not foreign to the Old Testament, it is virtually nonexistent in contexts where *ḥen* is used. Usually people asked God to locate something favorable in *themselves* as a reason for God to do something for them. In these settings asking God to find "favor" in us is similar to saying, "Dear God, if you like me, if I please you, hear my prayer."

But the verb "to be gracious/merciful" or "to show favor" *(ḥanan)* brings us much closer to the idea of "grace" with which we are the most familiar. This basic stem occurs 56 times in the Old Testament, 41 of which have Yahweh as the subject. In other words, God is the main biblical figure who shows mercy. So a frequent petition in the book of Psalms is that God might turn toward us "and be gracious." "Give me relief from my distress; be merciful [*ḥanan*] to me and hear my prayer" (Ps. 4:1b). Perhaps the single most famous use of this verb, and one that could be seen as foundational for all biblical requests for God's grace and mercy, is the great Aaronic benediction in Numbers 6:24-26:

"The LORD bless you
  and keep you;
the LORD make his face shine upon you
  and be gracious to you [*ḥanan*];
the LORD turn his face toward you
  and give you peace."

In these prayers, petitions, and blessings it would appear that while *ḥen/*"favor" is something to be found in people ("Find favor in me, O God"), the disposition to *show* favor or mercy is a possession of God ("Because you are merciful, please forgive me, I pray"). God was known to have this generous personality trait of mercy, and it was for this reason that the psalmists were encouraged to petition God for aid, rescue, strength, and so on. Those requests could be made with a fair measure of confidence precisely because God is gracious, because he is prone to show mercy. Just as you would not ask a poor man for money, so also you would not ask God for mercy if you did not already know that he was "rich in mercy." In addition, if God were "rich in mercy," but also had the reputation for being miserly or stingy with that mercy, you would be quite shy to ask for it. But if you knew that God was *both* rich in mercy *and* generously inclined to give it away, you would be quite quick to pray to God for precisely this needed gift of mercy and grace.

But where does this confidence in God's generous mercy giving come from? What was it about God that made Old Testament people think he was inclined to be gracious? The answer to these questions ushers us into a concept that in some ways lies at the heart of the Old Testament's theology of God, the attribute of God's "lovingkindness" (Heb. *ḥesed*).

The Hebrew word *ḥesed* (which virtually merges with *ḥen* in later Old Testament writings)[4] has been called a kind of "grace in relation" as God interacts with humanity.

Earlier we defined grace as a saving power of God that is rooted in his abiding love. The word and concept of God's *ḥesed* reveals the snug fit between the love of God and his penchant to show grace and mercy to sinners. In a sense *ḥesed* helps us to see that the grace of God is the powerful saving arm of his love.

4. Kittel and Friedrich, *Theological Dictionary of the New Testament*, p. 381.

17

The reason people could seek God's mercy, and have good hope of finding it, is precisely because the God of Israel was overflowing with lovingkindness. In Psalm 136 the Hebrew poet reels off a long list of evidences of God's greatness, from the creation to the redemption of Israel from Egypt. After each line he sings out the refrain, "His love endures forever." Actually, the key word of that refrain is rather ill translated as "love." The King James Version renders it "mercy," the Revised Standard Version has "steadfast love," but the American Standard Version perhaps comes closest to the mark with "lovingkindness." In any case, the Hebrew word in the refrain is *hesed,* which, while encompassing "love," is actually a much fuller, richer word.

From the viewpoint of the ancient Hebrews, this *hesed* of God is in some ways his root attribute; all of God's other attributes or personality traits flow from his lovingkindness. God's everlasting mercy, goodness, friendliness, and faithfulness — the very traits by which God moved Israel through salvation history — all stem from God's *hesed.* Indeed, the history of God's chosen people begins with Abraham and the covenant there established: "I will be your God and the God of your descendants after you" (Gen. 17:7b). Thereafter, God's covenantal relationship with Israel is founded upon and sustained by God's marvelous *hesed.* For this reason the word receives massive attention in the Psalter (it comes up 127 times in the 150 psalms) as that trait of Yahweh which most deserves the praise of his creatures. Psalm 48:9 provides a good one-sentence summary of the motivation behind the entire book of Psalms: "Within your temple, O God, / we meditate on your unfailing love [*hesed*]." Why do we praise God? Why do we pray to him for mercy? The Old Testament answer is that he is full of lovingkindness.

As frequently happens when a word gains such eminence, there are times when it is nearly personified or at least objectified. "Love [*hesed*] and faithfulness meet together; / righteousness and peace kiss each other" (Ps. 85:10). At the risk of exaggeration, it could be fairly said that, in the Hebrew mind, *hesed* is an excellent one-word summary of who God is. God's covenant, in which Israel finds her beginning and by which she sustains her hope, was founded upon God's lovingkindness.

Once Israel was founded as this covenant people, she frequently needed to be forgiven. This forgiveness, frequently granted even in the face of terrible wickedness, likewise spins out of God's lovingkindness,

18

out of his disposition to be merciful and not wrathful. A good example of this comes from Isaiah 54, where God admits his intense anger at Israel's horrible sins, but then concludes,

> "So now I have sworn not to be angry with you,
>   never to rebuke you again.
> Though the mountains be shaken
>   and the hills be removed,
> yet my unfailing love [ḥesed] for you will not be shaken
>   nor my covenant of peace be removed,
>   says the LORD, who has compassion on you." (Isa. 54:9b-10)[5]

While the lush fullness of New Testament grace is not found in the Old Testament, the Old Testament is by no means devoid of grace and its cognate themes and concepts. There can be little disputing that the Old Testament contains numerous laws, rituals, sacrifices, and holiness codes. Nor can there be much disputing that God frequently shows wrath in the Old Testament, both against his own people and the nations who oppose him. But it would be a shallow reading of the Old Testament to claim that only these themes are present or that their presence so dominates as to exclude any other considerations of grace, mercy, and lovingkindness.

The subtext of the entire Old Testament, its basic, underlying theological tenet, is that God is first and last a gracious God whose lovingkindness is the spring both for creation and for redemption. While the full salvific impact of the word "grace" is developed only in the New Testament writings of Paul, ideas and examples of grace drip off the pages of the Old Testament like honey. In a recent book on

5. In the Old Testament (e.g., Exod. 34:6; Ps. 89:14) God is routinely referred to as a God of *ḥesed we-emet* ("love and faithfulness," as the NIV renders it). When the Old Testament was translated into the Greek language around 300 B.C., *ḥesed we-emet* was rendered *charis kai alētheia* in the Greek. Later, John tells us in the prologue to his Gospel that Jesus is full of "grace and truth" (John 1:14). The Greek phrase that John used is none other than *charis kai alētheia,* thus creating an intriguing connection between the "grace"/*charis* of Christ in the New Testament and the "lovingkindness"/*ḥesed* of God so regularly celebrated in the Old Testament. Indeed, the same "lovingkindness" that so excited Old Testament believers became known as "grace" to New Testament believers. In Christ, God's lovingkindness will indeed endure forever.

grace, James Montgomery Boice claims that because the Old Testament is filled with laws, most of the people of the Old Testament saw God as "rather demanding, harsh, unbending, and judging."[6] Not so. The grace of God so eloquently celebrated in the New Testament was well known to the figures of the Old Testament under the heading of God's lovingkindness, which endures forever.

The grace of God begins already in Eden where, in the so-called "protoevangelium" or "pre-gospel," God looks at the trembling, twitching Adam and Eve, puts away the promise of death, and instead promises to send One who would make all things new. The grace of God is found in his initiation of the covenant with Abram as well as in his repeated forgiving of his people despite their routine breaking of their end of the bargain. God's words to David after his adultery and murder could well sum up the whole Old Testament witness: "The LORD has taken away your sin. You are not going to die" (2 Sam. 12:13).

Throughout the Old Testament the words of Aaron's benediction ring out, "'The LORD . . . be gracious to you; / the LORD turn his face toward you'" (Num. 6:25-26). One could almost say that it is God's repeated "turning toward" us in mercy that fuels the engine of his salvation. Time and again, despite wrenching evil and gross sinfulness, despite iniquity that stinks to the very height of heaven, God forgives. Over and again God turns toward his people, until one day God turned so sharply toward his people as to *turn into* one of them in Jesus the incarnate Christ. Only the power of God's grace, so deeply embedded in his love, could make such a turn possible. Only this same power could likewise transform us into a gracious people who live in imitation of this God as we are re-created in the image of the incarnate Christ.

Those who focus only on the law and wrath of the Old Testament (à la Marcion) find this last "turn" of God to be merely shocking. But those who pay close attention to the God whose "lovingkindness endures forever" find it merely consistent. This is but the ultimate grace of a God who has repeatedly been gracious until it hurt, the ultimate fulfillment of a promise made long ago with Abraham. In the everlasting grace of God, the incarnation and then the death of God's Son spell our very salvation. God saves us not because we deserve it but simply

---

6. James Montgomery Boice, *Amazing Grace* (Wheaton, IL: Tyndale Publishing House, Inc., 1993), p. 35.

because God is gracious enough to make the best thing in life free indeed.

We need to see next the development of "grace" in the writings of the New Testament. We will address the striking absence of the word "grace"/*charis* from the Gospels shortly, but first we will examine the later development of the concept because only then can we look back to see if that development was warranted by the life and teachings of Jesus (even if, as already noted, the word "grace" is itself lacking).[7]

Pauline Grace

Lewis Smedes once pointed out that when Paul would open or close a letter with the words "Grace be with you," he was actually using a tired little cliché. "Grace be with you" was the kind of phrase heard in pubs as people clinked their glasses in the ancient equivalent to "Cheers!" But when Paul said it, the words sparkled with new life and vigor. What was a tired commonplace in the rest of the ancient world became the central concept in Paul's theology of Jesus Christ. For if there is one word that captures Paul's understanding of salvation, "grace" is surely it.[8]

In order to appreciate the marvelous way in which Paul used this word, it would be helpful to examine first the ancient Greek uses of *charis*. In early Greek writings, *charis* could mean "favor" (similar to the Old Testament uses of *ḥen,* as noted above), but it could also refer to a kind of charm or pleasure. A "graceful" person was a charming person, someone with the kind of personality that could win friends and influence people. Among the original meanings of this word were notions of something delightful, something that brought joy or cheer to a person. Thus, a cognate form of *charis* is *chairo,* which can mean "to rejoice" or "to be full of joy." Good, beautiful, "gracious" objects

---

7. I am aware that the Gospels were actually written later than the writings of Paul; by speaking of Paul's "later development" of grace, I mean "later" in reference to Paul's work vis-à-vis Christ's life, not vis-à-vis the Gospels' composition.

8. Lewis B. Smedes, *How Can It Be All Right When Everything Is All Wrong?* (San Francisco: Harper and Row Publishers, Inc., 1982), p. 2.

brought delight and joy; they gladdened the heart and caused a person to rejoice in his or her good fortune.

Charis could also be associated with a person's (or a god's) attitude toward someone else. Even here the idea of "joy" is present in that if you had the "favor" of someone (especially of a god), then that was reason to rejoice and give thanks (the Greek word for "giving thanks" is *eucharistō,* which is also a cognate form of *charis*). In short, in the writings of the ancient Greeks words of delight and happiness and joy cluster around and cling to *charis* like iron filings on a magnet. Life's "graces" were what made life enjoyable, delightful, and charming. The presence of these graces was also that for which one gave thanks and in which one rejoiced.

Thus, although the word may have been something of a commonplace in Paul's day, one can certainly see in it the range of wonder, joy, and beauty that would come to be the hallmark of Paul's theological use of *charis.* Still, Paul's use of "grace" was unique and, in its own way, innovative. Unlike other religious notions in which "favor" is something to be found in the religious supplicant (either by earning it or by simply possessing it), Paul translated "grace" into something that evokes the deepest joy and the greatest thanksgiving because of the wondrous fact that it is a gift. Not only do we not deserve it, but we could never deserve it — it cannot be earned but only received. Gracious people, in Paul's view, are not those who are naturally charming or who have racked up sufficient merits so as to warrant a god's favor. No, gracious people are first of all "graced people," that is, people who are gracious in imitation of God only because they had first been *given* God's grace as a sheer, undeserved, surprise gift!

That grace is a gift must be our starting point in trying to understand "grace" as Paul understood and developed it. Unless we grasp this fundamental approach, unless we divorce grace from all notions of earnings or merits, nothing else we say about Paul could possibly be correct. Later we will have occasion to think about how very difficult this is for us to do, but for now suffice it to say that, for Paul, grace was free. Indeed, it had to be free and unearned or it could not be grace. "[We] are justified freely by his grace through the redemption that came by Christ Jesus" (Rom. 3:24). "[I]f by grace, then it is no longer by works; if it were, grace would no longer be grace" (Rom. 11:6).

But let us now move on into other areas of Pauline thought in order to see how he developed this basic idea. One can gain the broadest possible perspective on Paul's thought through the law versus grace debate. Traditionally many of us were taught that the Jews, especially the Pharisees, believed that they could keep the Law so perfectly that they could earn God's favor and thus deserved to be saved. Sometimes we have been taught to think of Paul as a kind of ancient Martin Luther.

Luther spent much of his early life in search of a gracious God. But Luther was taught by the church of his day that God was mostly interested in how well we keep his commandments. But the more Luther scrutinized his own life, the more he realized that he never kept God's Law perfectly — he always fell at least a little bit short (and usually he fell very far short). Luther's self-scrutiny extended unstintingly even to his own confessions of sin, which, he believed, were themselves so shot through with sin that even his prayers about sin pushed him into yet more sins, which also had to be confessed! Thus Luther never had peace, always had doubts, never felt certain that he was saved. But when Luther discovered the biblical teaching that we are saved by grace alone, he at long last could breathe easy and rejoice in God's salvation. It did not depend on his efforts after all — it was a gift. Luther's "Hallelujah!" over this truth continues to echo throughout the world.

Frequently we have been taught to see Paul as having the same kind of struggles. Paul, we have been told, was a Pharisee who also tried to save himself because that was what he had always been taught he had to do. Paul, and the other Pharisees of his day, believed that a person had to work his way to heaven through perfect keeping of the Law. But new scholarship on what the Pharisees taught and believed has cast doubt on the thesis that the Pharisees believed that only human works can save. Stephen Westerholm claims that in reality the Jews, including the Pharisees, did believe in God's grace but that it had become complicated and compromised by other teachings.[9]

Westerholm asserts that the Jews viewed their inclusion in the covenant community as being the basis of their salvation and that this inclusion, as noted above, was a result of God's lovingkindness or grace

9. Stephen Westerholm, *Israel's Law and the Church's Faith* (Grand Rapids: Eerdmans, 1988).

— grace was their starting point. But lawkeeping also had a very high profile in most Jewish circles as the way to *maintain* salvation or at very least somehow to contribute meaningfully to its possession or retention. In other words, the grace of God may have initiated the covenant, but the works of the Law were what kept that covenant well oiled and running smoothly.

Thus, when Paul was a Pharisee (his "blue period," as Frederick Buechner once put it), he saw the Law as a major player on the road to salvation. But after Paul was confronted with the living Lord Jesus Christ and the full impact of his death on the cross, he became convinced that there is only one way to salvation, and that is through grace, and grace *alone*. The Law has nothing to do with it. For the Law is all about doing, but salvation is all about receiving. The Law is all about who we are, salvation is all about who God is.[10] The Law, Paul then claimed, was never intended to save — it was at best our "custodian" until Christ should come to save us at last. Human efforts, even the best, could never accomplish in a lifetime what grace gives in an instant.

So what distinguished Paul from the Jews of his day, and from his own preconversion self, was not necessarily works versus grace but partial reliance on grace versus complete reliance on grace. If one relies on grace only partially while looking to lawkeeping to do the rest, that gives the Law a purpose that it was never intended to have (a saving one). Paul's later reliance on grace alone recognizes that if Christ had to die for us, then that can mean only that this, and this alone, was and always had been God's intended way to bring us back to himself. The Law had not failed in the sense of not having reached its intended goal (an idea related to a more dispensationalist view of history, which says that God kept trying different things to save us but that none of them worked until he finally had to send Jesus as a kind of last resort). The Law was never intended to save us.

One of the places where Paul lays this out most clearly is Galatians 3. There Paul tries to hash out how the Law fits into God's larger plan of salvation. As he tries to weed out the legalism that had begun to sprout in the Galatian churches, Paul makes clear that if lawkeeping were the way to God, then Christ died in vain — his death would be

---

10. Cf. Frederick Buechner, *Wishful Thinking* (New York: Harper and Row Publishers, Inc., 1973), p. 49.

a waste if there had been any chance of our getting to God by some other way in the first place.

But Paul also is at pains to find the proper "niche" for the Law. After all, it must have had some use and purpose. So he makes clear first of all that the covenant with Abraham had been established centuries before the Law was ever given. But if lawkeeping were the way to salvation, would it not it have been given *first?* Would not God have waited to see how well Abraham kept the law *before* he established a covenant with him? After all, you do not give someone a ticket to a football game *after* he is already sitting in the stadium munching on a hotdog! If the Law had been our entrance ticket to the kingdom, it would have been given before God brought us into relationship with himself.

Perhaps an analogy would help. Most parents eventually establish certain household rules that they hope their children will obey out of respect for Mom and Dad. But long before any such rules are given, parents love their children, give them bottles, change their diapers, and many other things. Love for the child comes first, and it will always be there (in healthy families anyway). The rules come later and are then part of the relationship, but they are not the basis of the parents' love — that was there to begin with. After all, what kind of parent would withhold love, would refuse to change a diaper or give a bottle, until the child could first show some obedience to a set of rules? Indeed, what child would ever survive if this were the way things worked!

So also with God: If lawkeeping were the basis of God's love, he would have given the laws first. But he did not. First he loved unconditionally; only later did he hand out some rules. So if the Law was never intended to save us or to bring us to God, what was its purpose? In Galatians 3:24 Paul uses a curious Greek word to describe the Law's function: *paidogōgos*. In the ancient world a *paidogōgos* was a slave who was given charge over a young boy. He would protect the boy from harm, bring him to school in the morning, escort him home in the afternoon, and so on. Perhaps the best modern-day equivalent would be a baby-sitter. The Law, Paul claims, was our baby-sitter. It took care of us, kept us in check, protected us, helped us to live in the design of the creation until that time when salvation would come finally and fully and graciously through Christ. The Law "took care" of us during the pre-Messiah time of history. It was our custodian or baby-sitter and as such was very important. But it was not and never could have been our Savior.

Now that Christ has come, Paul says, we are free from the Law. No, as we will make clear later, we are not "free from the Law" in the sense of being able to live however we want. But we are free in the sense of no longer being watched over by a baby-sitter. We have matured to a new stage of humanity's relationship with God. It is a stage of being "in Christ," the full implications of which need careful, thoughtful attention (especially regarding the Law's place in the life of those saved by grace). But for now it is clear that, contrary to what he had been taught in the school of the Pharisees, Paul came to believe that there was only one road that led to God, and that was the road of grace — the road blazed by our Pioneer, Jesus Christ.

Thus we are back to grace alone as the power of God that is lavished on us as a sheer, undeserved, loving gift of the Almighty. If we think that our works contribute to our salvation in any way, whether before the fact of grace or after its reception, we drift from Paul's uncompromising position of grace *alone*. Unfortunately, as we will note in Chapter Two, our temptation most typically is not to think we are saved by what we do — because that is so obviously wrong — but rather to adopt the Pharisees' way of thinking that the gracious lives that result from grace help us to *stay* saved. Like the Pharisees (properly understood), we may acknowledge grace as getting us started in salvation, but then we look to living a "good life" to take us the rest of the way. But to Paul's mind claiming that our works help get us saved is just as bad as claiming that they save us completely. Either way, God's powerful grace gets short-circuited.

Paul's Damascus road epiphany and conversion shape and inform every sentence in Paul's later writings. While Paul was a staunch defender of the need to live a grateful life of spiritual fruit-bearing, while he recognized the need to be a "new creation" in Christ, he bristled every time he heard someone say the words "Grace *and*. . . ." The only thing Paul would permit after the word "grace" was a period or, better yet, an exclamation point! Paul's message was always one of grace, and grace alone. Anything less, anything more, was to turn the precious cross of Christ into a sham (Gal. 2:21).

By its very definition grace would be completely unnecessary, as would Christ's horrid death, if any other route to salvation were available. To say, "Grace and . . ." would be as inane as to say, "Free for $1." If we are truly saved by grace, as Paul understood grace, everything else in the Christian life is a result of grace, not a forerunner to it, not a contributor to it, not a coworker with it. Christ's death did not accomplish most of salvation or half of salvation but all of it. The only part we have to play is to receive the benefit of that full, rich salvation as a free gift of God's electing grace. The only way the good news of the gospel could be good would be if grace were just this free, just this undeserved, just this amazing.

Thus, all the secular nuances of the word *charis* met and twined together in Paul's thought in a most lovely way. Grace was the source of Paul's rejoicing, it was his highest delight, it was the only true source of his thanksgiving and the only thing that could ever bring him or anyone else a sense of holy cheer.

With all of that as the broad background to Paul's thought, let us now briefly survey a couple of specific texts to see how this gets fleshed out. The logical place to begin is the letter to the Romans, which contains the largest single concentration of references to *charis* in the New Testament (21 occurrences). In Romans we discover that while grace has a singular focus (saving us), it also is a many-faceted divine power. Grace is in fact so big that it warrants its own place on the cosmic map. Although the phrase "in Christ" is Paul's chief way of referring to salvation, he also frequently used "grace" in a kind of locative sense, as when he wrote that believers are "standing in grace" (Rom. 5:2) as though grace were its own place — specifically a place created by Christ's death and resurrection. In this sense, grace is a kind of "safe house" for wounded and battered souls.

But the core of grace in Romans (and everywhere else) is that it is God's powerful gift whereby the perfection of Christ is transferred into our spiritual accounts. In the poem "As Kingfishers," Gerard Manley Hopkins captures this central facet of grace nicely with the words,

> the just man justices; Keeps grace:
>   that keeps all his goings graces;
> Acts in God's eye what in God's eye he is —
>   Christ.

Grace is that power and gift of God by which he lays our sin on Jesus but then also lays Jesus' righteousness on us such that when God looks at us, he sees only Christ. Theologically this is the doctrine of justification. God removes our sin, replaces it with Christ's perfect righteousness, and so places us in a right relationship once again with himself.

Frederick Buechner once used the analogy of page justifications. If the words on a page are "right justified," that means that each line ends at the same point along an invisible vertical line along the right margin. The sentences are thus flush with, and thus stand in a proper relationship to, the straight edge of the paper. So also with our relationship to God. Sin so offends God's holiness that its presence in us caused our relationship with him to become jagged and frayed. We were unjustified sinners incapable of coming into a right relationship with a God of unspeakable holiness. But when God gives us the righteousness of Christ, our lives line up with the righteous holiness of God himself, thus restoring our broken and jagged relationship. God has justified us in Christ, thus restoring our lost relationship.[11]

Paul uses a number of locutions to communicate this, the sum total of which again drives home the all-inclusive nature of grace. Sometimes we are justified by grace (an instrumental dative in Rom. 3:24). At other times Paul says that we are ushered *into* grace (the more locative view just mentioned). Yet another common expression is *under* grace as opposed to under the law (cf. Rom. 6:14ff.). So whereas once we were in sin, in the flesh, in the world, grace came as God's power that places us in Christ, in the Spirit, in the kingdom of God where, as full citizens, we now dwell securely.

This grace of God, in Paul's view, is always more than a match for the sin to which it stands in opposition. This is so simply because grace springs from the inestimable power of Christ and thus always rises to the challenge. Grace always drowns sin in a floodtide of divine goodness because, in Christ, grace superabounds to those who need it most, namely, sinners.

But what is the hookup of believers to this grace? Faith. It could be said that faith is the vessel or the container that holds grace. Faith is the pipeline that brings this cleansing floodtide into a believer's soul. Faith is the wire that conducts the power of God's grace into the circuitry of the person. But if we think that faith is a human artifact that we achieve on our own, that would mean that we do contribute

11. Buechner, *Wishful Thinking*, pp. 48-49.

something and so help grace along after all. To avoid this, Paul also makes clear that faith is itself grace's first gift. Even the container that holds grace is given to us by grace!

As Augustine once put it, "To desire the help of grace is the beginning of grace."[12] In other words, even faith cannot be credited to our accounts because faith is the gift by which we enjoy the gift. If God did not give us faith, we would never receive grace. In this sense, faith is like a TV antenna. As you read these words, the air around you is filled with television signals. But you do not notice them, and you certainly cannot decipher them, because they simply are bouncing off you or passing through you. Your brain lacks the necessary antenna equipment to pull them in. So, too, the "signals" of God's grace fill the cosmos, but unless we are given faith these grace signals simply bounce off our souls meaninglessly. Faith is like an antenna for the soul that pulls in grace's signal, focuses it, and then projects it onto the screen of our souls, allowing us to view and enjoy the gospel story and its truth for our lives.

Throughout the rest of the Pauline corpus, these basic ideas are repeated over and over in a multitude of ways but always with the same basic thrust: grace alone through faith alone (Eph. 2:7-8). Grace's first gift, faith, is that which then enables us to recognize in Christ and in the "foolishness" of his cross the very wisdom of God by which, and only by which, we are saved (cf. 1 Cor. 1:18-19).

Given all that, we can see that when Paul opened a letter saying "Grace and peace be unto you," he was using no cliché! For Paul took this little Greek phrase and poured marvelous new meaning into it. For Paul, "Grace be unto you" was the ultimate cosmic "Cheers!" *Charis* glistens with meaning in Paul's writings because it glistened with meaning in Paul's life. As noted above, prior to his conversion Paul was not a Luther-like seeker for a gracious God. But he was quite zealous in keeping the Law in that he was sure it had something to do with getting him into God's kingdom. But after the reality of the cross was shown to him through his new eyes of faith, graciously given to him by God, he saw clearly for the first time that if salvation does not come to us as a gift, it does not come to us at all.

12. Augustine, "On Grace and Free Will," in *The Nicene and Post-Nicene Fathers,* ed. Philip Schaff (Grand Rapids: Eerdmans, 1987), V, 472.

Although it would be possible to nuance all of this in slightly varying ways, it would be difficult for any New Testament reader to miss these salient features of Paul's thought. But now we need to address the seeming contradiction raised earlier in this chapter, namely, what about the Gospels? If Paul makes such a massive use of grace, indeed, if "grace" for Paul is a one-word summary of the gospel, how are we to account for the lack of "grace" in the very accounts that tell us the gospel story? It is to this vital question that we now turn.

Grace in the Gospels?

Before getting specific, we should note that only a narrow, literalistic approach to the Bible would insist on being able to find the word *charis*/"grace" in Matthew, Mark, Luke, or John in order to warrant claiming that the Gospels are in fact all about grace. Even as we ought not to be shaken by the Jehovah's Witness tactic of pointing out that the word "Trinity" does not occur in the Bible, so also we ought to allow the process of interpretation enough latitude to find grace in places where the word proper may not be spelled out for us. Indeed, this must be our approach to the Gospels because the cold, hard fact is that, with the exception of Luke 2:40, "grace" does not appear in the Synoptic Gospels (and even Luke 2:40 uses "grace" in a very different sense from what one finds in Paul).

But assuming Paul was well versed in the stories and teachings of Jesus (and we will assume that here, even though many scholars hotly dispute this assertion), the question to be asked is this: Do the stories and teachings of Christ naturally lead to Paul's later systematic statements about grace, or are there hints that what Jesus was really all about was actually something quite different? To return to our earlier "puzzle" analogy, do Jesus' life and teaching contain pieces of the larger picture of grace, or are even such scattered pieces absent from the Gospels? As even a brief survey of the Gospels will show, everything about Jesus does indeed proclaim the gospel of grace no less eloquently and no less certainly than do the writings of Paul. When Paul later put the big picture of grace together, he was indeed picking up various "puzzle pieces" from the Gospels.

To demonstrate the truth of that bold assertion, we will survey first Jesus' clashes with the Pharisees and all he had to say about the Law. Then we will examine the parables of Jesus, both those that Jesus spoke in his sermons and the "acted out" parables of Jesus' ordinary, day-to-day interactions with those around him.

First, Jesus, the Law, and the Pharisees. The logical place to begin on this subject is the locus classicus of Matthew 5:17-20.[13] When one thinks of Jesus and his relationship to the Pharisees, the most immediate words and images that spring to mind are very adversarial in nature. One thinks of Jesus lambasting the Pharisees as "white-washed graves," as people who look good on the outside but who stink of spiritual death and decay on the inside. It is easy and natural to reflect on all those times when Jesus said or did something that left the Pharisees fuming in self-righteous anger, causing them to turn their backs and begin plotting against Jesus. In short, the most common caricature is that of Jesus being the freewheeling libertine who played fast and loose with the Law of God while the Pharisees were the nit-picking legalists for whom the Law of God had to remain inviolate.

Yet in what may be the single most important passage on Jesus and the Law, it is striking to find Jesus recommending that true believers have a brand of righteousness that actually *exceeds* that of the Pharisees. In the Sermon on the Mount, Jesus takes pains to clarify that his ministry will not annul or destroy the Law of God (something that ought to have calmed the troubled spirit of many a Pharisee), but it would aim, rather, to fulfill that very Law.

How are we to understand the seeming ambiguity between what Jesus says in Matthew 5 and the overt clashes Jesus has with the Pharisees in the rest of the Gospels? Is Jesus for the Law or against it? If he is for it, then what is the actual distinction between himself and the Pharisees? Also, where does all of this leave the grace with which we are most concerned in this study? We have already noted that the actual word

---

13. Although I nowhere quote from it directly, I wish to acknowledge in general Frederick Dale Bruner, whose twin commentaries on Matthew, *The Christbook, Matthew 1–12* (Waco: Word Books, 1987) and *The Churchbook, Matthew 13–28* (Dallas: Word Publishing, 1990), have made invaluable contributions to my thinking about Matthew's Gospel. Much of my insight into Matthew in the pages ahead probably had its origin somewhere in Bruner's outstanding commentaries.

"grace" is absent from Jesus' teachings and life narratives, but was the concept also lacking? What was Jesus' primary focus? Law, works, grace?

Let us try to untangle this knot of questions by looking at the Sermon on the Mount, most especially Matthew 5:17-20. The first point we need to note is simple yet foundational: The Sermon on the Mount is *not* a series of kingdom entrance requirements. It is easy to misread this most famous of Jesus' sermons. After all, when Jesus says, "Blessed are the peacemakers, / for they will be called sons of God" (Matt. 5:9), it is easy to read that as, "If you make peace, you will become a son of God in the kingdom." So, too, with the rest of the sermon: All of Jesus' words about the commandments of God, all of Jesus' various beatitudes, all of Jesus' warnings and words about fasting and praying — all of them sound like prerequisites for kingdom inclusion. It is as though Jesus were saying, "If you do this or act this way, you will be saved."

If Jesus had delivered this sermon to the masses, this would be a possible (though not necessary) conclusion. However, the one point we most frequently miss is the way in which this Sermon begins. To whom is Jesus preaching? Matthew 5:1-2 makes clear that Jesus in fact turned *away* from the crowds, faced his disciples, and then taught *them*. Why is this important to notice? Because the disciples were the ones who were, in a sense, already "in" the kingdom of God. Jesus was "preaching to the choir" in this great sermon. Thus the string of "Blessed are" statements are not intended to mean "You *will be* blessed if you do such and so," but rather "Congratulations! Blessed are you because you *are* such and so."[14]

Seen in this light, therefore, the Sermon on the Mount is not a "How To" manual for getting into God's favor, but a series of commands and recommendations and blessings for those *already* in God's favor simply because God had graciously called them to come in ("Follow me!"). These are the exercises and lifestyles of those who have already been touched and called by God's Spirit. So this is somewhat similar to Paul's point about Abraham and the Law: The relationship came first; the rules came later. The disciples had already been called in by grace; these various regulations were how they were to behave now that they were in God's kingdom.

14. Dr. David Holwerda of Calvin Theological Seminary first alerted me to this angle on the Sermon.

It is imperative that we see the Sermon on the Mount in this light lest we draw false conclusions from Jesus' words. Likewise Matthew 5:17-20 must be read from this angle.

> "Do not think that I have come to abolish the Law or the Prophets; I have not come to abolish them but to fulfill them. I tell you the truth, until heaven and earth disappear, not the smallest letter, not the least stroke of a pen, will by any means disappear from the Law until everything is accomplished. Anyone who breaks one of the least of these commandments and teaches others to do the same will be called least in the kingdom of heaven, but whoever practices and teaches these commands will be called great in the kingdom of heaven. For I tell you that unless your righteousness surpasses that of the Pharisees and the teachers of the law, you will certainly not enter the kingdom of heaven."

Within the kingdom of God, Jesus has not come to abolish the Law but to fulfill it. Actually, what Jesus says is not that he came to fulfill the Law, but the Law and the Prophets, that is, the Scriptures in toto! It is highly significant that Jesus adds the words "or the Prophets," for by doing so he widens the scope from a narrow focus on legalistic commands to the broader warp and woof of the Scriptures. Already here we find a difference between Jesus' perspective and that of the Pharisees. For although the prophets also spoke much about the Law (and while they, of course, respected the Law of God exceedingly highly), they pointed as well to a new era in which the Law would take on a different hue. For the prophets, then, the Law was never the end of the story, but just the beginning. (This point accords with what we pointed out above when we said that the Law was a baby-sitter prior to final salvation, not salvation itself.)

The grandest passage in this regard is Jeremiah 31, where we are told that a time would come, the time of the New Covenant, when the Law of God would be written not on stone tablets (à la Moses at Sinai) but on the fleshy tablets of human hearts. Jeremiah seems to indicate that a time would come (and in Jesus did come) when the Law of God would switch from being an external set of demands to being an internal moral compass. This is the common Age of Salvation motif, which is woven all through the Old Testament prophets as they looked forward to and anticipated the Messiah, who would fundamentally fulfill all of God's covenantal purposes for Israel and, indeed, for the entire world.

That is why throughout the Prophets one can find the "all nations" idea; in other words, the Messiah would come and would then be a blessing not only to Israel but to all the nations of the earth. Isaiah 56:6-7 is a good example of this idea of internationalizing even the temple of God:

> "And foreigners who bind themselves to the LORD
>   to serve him,
> to love the name of the LORD,
>   and to worship him . . .
> these I will bring to my holy mountain
>   and give them joy in my house of prayer . . .
> for my house will be called
>   a house of prayer for all nations."[15]

Jesus alludes to this through his simple inclusion of the words "or the Prophets." A key difference between Jesus and the Pharisees was this: The Pharisees focused only on the Law of God and its various commands (to which they had added many more subcommands). They then strove to fulfill these commands as perfectly as they could. They did so because this was viewed as the necessary precursor of and prerequisite to the visible coming of God's kingdom.

A person had to keep the Law fully to be saved (for such lawkeeping fulfilled the human half of the salvation bargain). With so much at stake, it is not surprising that a furious form of legalism developed. After all, the very coming of the kingdom to earth was on

---

15. This text from Isaiah 56, along with another text from Jeremiah 7, was quoted by Jesus after his Triumphal Entry when he was cleansing the temple of the moneychangers. Because the moneychangers had set up their oriental bazaar and flea market in the Gentile Court of the Temple, the Gentiles had no place in the temple in which to pray. So Jesus makes room for them, recognizing that the fullness of their inclusion was at hand. Once again, the Pharisees' exclusive focus on the Law caused them to ignore the words of the Prophets about the inclusion of "all nations." They were so sure that keeping the Law would bring the Messiah to them that they forgot that the Messiah would open the gates of salvation graciously to include the Gentiles as well.

the line! Therefore, anyone who threatened the pure maintenance of this Law was anathematized as being Antichrist. This is why whenever Jesus appeared to be breaking the strict letter of the Law (as in the various Sabbath controversies), the Pharisees concluded that Jesus could not be the Messiah — no one who broke the Law could possibly be the Messiah because it was the very *keeping* of the Law that would *bring* the Messiah!

Jesus took another view. Jesus pointed to the Age of Salvation as presented by the Prophets. In Jesus' view, this age did not and could not come about as a result of human effort (that had never been the Law's purpose, as Paul later wrote) but could only come about as a gift of God. Once that gracious gift is given, once one is included in the kingdom of God through the grace of God, one could take a fresh approach to the Law of God, which is precisely what Jesus is doing in the Sermon on the Mount: He is addressing those already in the kingdom by grace and then saying, "Now that you're in, here's how you should think about the Law."

So from this perspective, what is Jesus saying when he recommends a righteousness that "surpasses" that of the Pharisees? Simply put, Jesus is saying that nothing is wrong with the Law — it does trace out for us the shape of the obedient life before God. Where the Pharisees went wrong, however, was in thinking that while God's "grace" had elected them into the kingdom, their perfect keeping of the Law would both maintain their status in the kingdom and help usher in the visible kingdom when the Messiah would come to establish his rule over Israel. But, according to Jesus, keeping the Law is not how you get into God's kingdom, nor is it a way to maintain your status in the kingdom. The life of the kingdom is grace from first to last. The Law needs to be respected and followed very carefully only because it is the blueprint of the gracious life that characterizes those touched by God's grace. Lawkeeping is the *result* of salvation by grace, not the precursor to it, nor the maintainer of it.

As Jeremiah predicted, once engrafted into God's kingdom, you would have the Law written on your very heart, which would seem to be another way of saying that God would enable you to keep the Law on a deeper level than the superficial ways of legalistic, Pharisaic lawkeeping. The Pharisees kept the Law only externally in order to gain something else. But true disciples keep the Law not in a quid-pro-quo attempt to get something in return but simply as a natural, gracious, lovely result of God's saving activity in Christ. Once you are a citizen in God's kingdom by God's grace, you quite naturally act distinctively.

This explains the subsequent internalizing and radicalizing of the Ten Commandments, which follow immediately on Matthew 5:20. Jesus actually makes the Law more difficult to keep by saying things like, "It's not enough not to commit adultery; you must also keep your thoughts pure. It's not enough not to slip a knife between your brother's ribs; you've got to avoid becoming angry with him and calling him dirty names, too." All through the Sermon on the Mount, far from dumping the Law in favor of some kind of libertinism, Jesus intensifies and deepens the Law.

This radicalizing of the commandments had two effects: First, it proved that no human person could keep the Law perfectly. By making the Law so impossible to keep, Jesus was subtly rebuking those who thought outward appearances were the be-all and end-all of the Law. Second, Jesus deepened the Law to reveal the kind of obedience that God desires — an obedience that could become possible only by grace and the greater power which only grace could provide. That is why, if anyone had interrupted Jesus to ask who could possibly do all this, Jesus would have likely replied (as he did reply on other occasions), "With man this is impossible, but with God all things are possible." Salvation is a gift, not a reward — even keeping the Law as God truly intended it to be kept is not a human precursor to grace but only and always a *result* of grace. Grace is our spiritual root, and lawkeeping is the spiritual fruit that flows from and is nourished by that root.

The "greater righteousness" required of disciples, therefore, issued from the relationship believers would have as a result of God's new covenant established by the Messiah in the fullness of time, in the Age of Salvation foreseen by the Prophets of old. Anyone who focused on the Law of God to the exclusion of the Prophets would be unable to see in Jesus the coming of this age and thus in Jesus the presence of the Messiah.

As Paul wrote in 2 Corinthians 3:7-18, those who look to the faded glory of the Law as the way to salvation are like people with a blanket over their heads. The real glory of the Messiah was right in front of them, but they could not see it because all their attention was focused on Mount Sinai and the giving of the Ten Commandments. They were stuck in history, unable to move along the road to salvation. Just as people sitting under a wool blanket cannot be impressed by even the most spectacular fireworks display, so the Jews whose spiritual eyesight was veiled by the Law could not be impressed by the real glory of Jesus the Christ.

So do Jesus' words about the Law and his interactions with the Pharisees confirm or deny the message of salvation by grace alone as it is affirmed in the rest of the New Testament? This whirlwind survey of Jesus and the Law demonstrates that while the word "grace" may be missing from the Gospel narratives, the concept is firmly in place. Living a certain lifestyle, keeping the commandments, or racking up a certain number of points is not the way into the kingdom. The Age of Salvation foretold by the Prophets comes by way of a divine gift. True, once one is a disciple of Jesus through the invitation of grace ("Follow me!"), a righteous lifestyle of obedience ought to ensue — but that is the fruit of God's saving activity, not the root. Those who focus on lawkeeping as salvation's root will not only miss seeing the arrival of the Messiah and his salvation, but they may even tragically miss receiving this Messiah.

Other passages regarding Jesus and the Pharisees could be multiplied to back this up, but perhaps one more will suffice. In Matthew 16:5-12, Jesus warns his disciples against "the leaven of the Pharisees." Once Jesus helped the disciples realize that he was not talking about literal bread (Jesus had enormous patience with those poor disciples!), he made it clear that by "leaven" he meant the teachings of the Pharisees.

But then Jesus did a curious thing: He connected this saying with his previous mass feedings of the 5,000 and the 4,000. Why did he do this? What is the connection? Perhaps this: Those feedings were fulfillments of the prophetic word that, when the Messiah came, it would be an age of fullness, of superabundance. Matthew and Mark's accounts of these miracles include words and details that present Jesus as the great shepherd who feeds his sheep in fulfillment of Old Testament prophecy. But the Pharisees, focusing as they were on the wrong things (the Law alone), missed seeing this messianic sign. Those who insist on working their way into the kingdom, those who insist on bringing the kingdom into existence through their conduct relative to the Law, miss seeing that the kingdom has already arrived as a sheer gift — all they need to do is accept this and hear the master calling to his sheep, "Follow me."

But let us leave aside the nascent, subtle grace of Jesus in his conflicts with the Pharisees and turn to what may be a more overt "grace feature" in Jesus' ministry: his parables. Although it is difficult to make neat distinctions of parable types, it can fairly be said that Jesus told three kinds of parables: Parables of the Kingdom, Parables of Grace, and Parables of Judgment (see Robert Capon's series of books by these very titles). It is the second type upon which we will focus. Two examples of this type of parable will suffice: The Parable of the Laborers in the Vineyard and the Parable of the Prodigal Son.

One parable that particularly helps make clear the nature of salvation as grace is the Parable of the Laborers in the Vineyard (Matt. 20:1-16). The story is scandalously simple: A vineyard owner is pressed hard by a harvest deadline and so hires workers throughout the course of a day to get the job done on time. At four different hours of the workday, from the crack of dawn to an hour before quitting time, the man hires workers and sends them out into the field. When the day is over and the workers line up to be paid, everyone is amazed that each worker receives the same pay. Well, not everyone is amazed — a good many are angry! "I worked out there for twelve hours! How in the world can someone who worked one hour get the same amount of money as I do?" When the owner hears this grumbling, his reply is simple, "I can pay whatever I want to whomever I want. I promised you a full day's wages and you're getting it. If I decide also to pay a full day's wage to these others, what is that to you? I'm a generous man; don't begrudge me that!"

Matthew then includes the line, "The last will be first, and the first will be last." In other words, God does not calculate merit, he gives goodness away to the least likely of people. He approaches whomever he chooses (including those whom no one else wanted — why else would they still have been unemployed one hour before quitting time?) and then "rewards" all of them the same. Those who work hard in the blazing sun for hours and so harvest tremendous amounts of fruit are fine people, but so are the ones who managed to bring in only a half-bushel. The work we do is wonderful, important, and highly appreciated, but it is not the basis on which we are "paid."

In short theological strokes: It is by grace that we are saved, not by works. Works are fine things in the kingdom, but we are not paid for them. We are paid because we were chosen, and we were chosen for no reason in particular other than that the master is generous.[16]

This idea comes home with equal clarity in the famed Parable of the Prodigal Son from Luke 15. As Luke 15 opens, Jesus is attending a dinner party thrown by "tax collectors and sinners." The Pharisees are outside muttering into their beards about this fellow Jesus and the lousy, sinful company he keeps. So Jesus tells a story about a man who has two sons, the younger of whom insults his father mightily by cashing in on his inheritance before his father dies. Many commentators have pointed out that the son's petition was essentially a request that the father "drop dead" in a legal sense so that the will could be put into effect. It was a horrible thing to request, so horrible that this may be the only example in all of Middle Eastern literature of such an incident between a father and son.[17]

When the inevitable happens and this younger son loses it all through wild living, he goes back home armed with a well-rehearsed line of confession: "Father, I have sinned against heaven and against you. I am no longer worthy to be called your son; make me like one of your hired men." But the hilarity of God's grace is seen best in this parable when the father tosses dignity to the wind, races out to meet his son, clobbers him not with anger but with joy, and instantly reinstates the lad to full sonship. The confession of sin is never even heard! By the time the bewildered son manages to blurt out the first line of his memorized confession, he has already been made back into a full son. He is clothed with the "best" robe (which was almost certainly his father's own robe), he is emblazoned again with the family seal through

16. Anyway, as Barbara Brown Taylor points out in an excellent sermon, why do we always read this parable from the perspective of those who worked the longest? Why do we so cozily assume that we are among those who worked for twelve hours? Maybe in God's eyes we are closer to the one-, two-, or three-hour workers. In that case we would have less reason to grumble about this generous owner and more reason to sing! See *A Chorus of Witnesses: Model Sermons for Today's Preacher,* ed. Thomas Long and Cornelius Plantinga, Jr. (Grand Rapids: Eerdmans, 1994), pp. 12-20.

17. Kenneth E. Bailey, *Poet and Peasant* (Grand Rapids: Eerdmans, 1976), p. 164.

the signet ring that is placed on his hand, and he is elevated above the level of a servant by having shoes placed on his feet *by* the servants who, in those days, always went barefoot.

The "Pharisee" makes a cameo appearance in this parable in the person of the older brother. He hears of all this gracious hoopla and is fit to be tied. When his father asks him what is wrong, he bitterly points out that his brother deserves none of this, whereas he had been "slaving away" for years but never had so much fuss made over his fine efforts. Once again Jesus points out that it is not what we do that counts, but what God does. The work we do for God is wonderful (though if we view it as a "slaving away" in order to curry God's favor, we demonstrate a wholesale lack of awareness that salvation is a gift), but it does not save. Likewise, the sins we commit (à la the younger son) are horrible and unspeakable, but if God wills to save us anyway, those sins cannot keep us out of the kingdom.

When Luke 15 opened, the Pharisees were pouting on the porch, complaining bitterly that Jesus kept company with all the wrong people. Since they saw keeping the law as the way to bring the Messiah, any Jew who hung around with lawbreakers was hindering the arrival of the kingdom. Jesus makes, to say the least, a rather different point! It is precisely because of "sinners" that salvation comes as a gift. If all one sees is lawkeeping and "slaving away," not only will one miss discovering that happy fact, but one will even miss out on the party that is God's kingdom. As the parable ends, the father is pleading with his older son to join the party for his wayward brother. The reader is then left to ponder whether or not he will. The choice is clear-cut — stay on the porch and pout, or go in to join the celebration. The one option is sheer joy; the other, absolute hell!

These two parables highlight, as well as anything in the Gospels, the very truths that Paul and the other New Testament writers would later systematize in their theological epistles. In and through everything Jesus taught, it was clear that the basis of our acceptance into God's favor has nothing to do with who we are, how we have behaved, or whether we keep the Law in a certain fashion, but simply and solely with the character of God as the generous vineyard owner, the ludicrously forgiving father, the Almighty One of the cosmos, "whose lovingkindness abides forever."

Earlier we noted that Jesus told many parables, but he also presented many "parables without words" through the ways in which he related to people. The sheer facts that Jesus would sup with prostitutes, converse lovingly with a Samaritan woman at a well, invite himself over to the house of Zacchaeus, forgive on the spot the woman caught in adultery, and speak the gospel to the thief on the cross all point to the fact that Jesus, the Word of God made flesh, was the very incarnation of grace.

It was no accident (nor was it any surprise) that Jesus so violently upset the teachers and keepers of the Law. Give the Pharisees credit for recognizing that if Jesus were the way, the truth, and the life, their way, their truth, and their path to life were wrong. Give the Pharisees their due inasmuch as they knew that if, as he claimed, Jesus was revealing the true character of God, that meant the harsh, strict, bookkeeping God of the Pharisees must have been a smear on the real thing.

So should we be disturbed at the paucity of the word "grace" in the four Gospels? Not at all! For those with eyes to see and minds to understand, grace is the golden thread that weaves its way through the entire warp and woof of the New Testament and, in fact, throughout that seamless garment known as Holy Scripture, Old and New Testaments alike.

Having surveyed Scripture's witness to the power of God's grace and the loving way in which it saves us, we are now poised to consider how this same power also transforms our lives into something gracious. For as we noted in the Introduction, the power of God's grace does not end merely in forgiving our sins; it also aims to change our lives. So how does being gracious tie in with being grateful (Chapter Two)? How do both grace and graciousness become threatened by our society's capitalist ethos (Chapter Three)? How does being gracious help us when facing one another's sins in the process of church discipline (Chapter Four)? These are the vital questions of the gracious life to which we will shortly turn.

Summary

The story is told that, many years ago, a conference was convened to discuss the study of comparative religions. Theologians and experts from various fields of religious studies gathered from all over the world to tackle certain knotty questions relating to Christianity and its similarities or dissimilarities to other faiths. One particularly interesting seminar was held to determine whether there was anything unique about the Christian faith. A number of Christianity's features were put on the table for discussion. Was it the incarnation? No; other religions also had various versions of the gods coming down in human form. Might it be the resurrection? No, various versions of the dead rising again were found in other faiths as well.

On and on the discussion went without any resolution in sight. At some point, after the debate had been underway for a time, C. S. Lewis wandered in late. Taking his seat, he asked a colleague, "What's the rumpus about?" and was told that they were seeking to find Christianity's unique trait among the world's religions. In the straightforward, no-nonsense, commonsense approach that was to make Lewis famous, he immediately said, "Oh, that's easy. It's grace." As the other scholars thought about that for a moment, they concluded that Lewis was right: It is grace. No other religion had ever made the ultimate acceptance by the Almighty so absolutely unconditional. In other faiths, there is usually some notion of earning points. Whether it was karma, Buddhist-like steps along the path to serenity, or some similar system, the idea was that to receive the favor of the gods one had to *earn* the favor of the gods.[18]

Not so in Christianity, at least not in true Christianity. True, the churches that proclaim the gospel's message have not (and still do not) always remembered this very well. But that the core of the gospel is grace can scarcely be disputed by anyone who takes the time to trace this theme carefully from Genesis to Revelation. The God "whose lovingkindness endures forever" is the same God who became man, lived, died, and rose again so as to make the best thing in life free.

There are many different ways of putting this central truth about grace. But whether one is thinking about Abraham, Jacob, David, Isaiah, Jesus, or the disciples, one would be hard pressed to do better than the simple but glorious words of Paul: "For it is by grace you have been saved, through faith — and this not from yourselves, it is the gift of God" (Eph. 2:8).

18. I heard this anecdote told in a speech on Lewis given at Calvin College by Lewis scholar Peter Kreeft.

MEDITATION

Grief and Grace

GENESIS 6–9

EVEN IN THIS TIME of profound biblical illiteracy, most people still know about "Noah's Ark." The image of the Ark pops up frequently in advertisements, as when brokerage firms are pictured as "arks of refuge" during stormy financial times. Also, one of Bill Cosby's comedy routines is a humorous retelling of the Noah story. And every couple of years the news is abuzz with the latest attempt to scale Mount Ararat "In Search of Noah's Ark."

It is a story that we all know — or think we do. But it is a story the crux of which is easily missed. For within the broader movement of these familiar chapters the careful Bible reader will detect a change taking place within God. Seeing the way in which God changes through the events of the Flood can help us understand what "Noah's Ark" is all about.

Although most people picture the God of the Flood as an angry, enraged deity, the biblical text paints a rather different portrait. The Flood that God sent comes not from an irrational, wild-eyed divine fury, but from a tragically broken divine heart. Genesis 6:6 sums it up well: "The LORD was grieved . . . and his heart was filled with pain."

The text tells us that God looked at his wonderful creation and, behold, it was ruined. In Genesis 1 we are told over and over that "God saw, and, behold, it was very good." In Genesis 6 we hear a sad echo of that as God sees and, behold, it is ruined! So in bitter sorrow God decides to start again.

But there is still too much good to wipe out everything — there

43

is, for instance, Noah. In righteous Noah, God sees the chance for renewal. So by preserving Noah, his family, and the various creatures of the earth, God tries to scour away some of sin's filth. When it is all over, God brings Noah out of the ark, reaffirms his love for the creation, and repeats the Genesis 1 command to "be fruitful and multiply."

But somewhere between Genesis 6 and Genesis 8 God changes. In Genesis 6:5 the narrator tells us, "The LORD saw how great man's wickedness on the earth had become, and that every inclination of the thoughts of his heart was only evil all the time." In chapter 6 God's grief over this evil leads to the Flood. But in Genesis 8:21 God says, "Never again will I curse the ground because of man, *for* every inclination of his heart is evil from childhood" (my translation and emphasis). These two texts are in nearly identical wording, but God's reactions are quite different.

In Genesis 6 God observes evil and uses it as a reason to destroy. In Genesis 8 God views the exact same evil and uses it as a reason to save. Something in God changed. The world was not different after the Flood, but God was. While we may not be able to account for this change fully, this story teaches us something vital, namely, that sin is serious business that evokes two responses from God: grief unto punishment and grace unto salvation.

The story of the Flood teaches that God's response to sin is not simply of grace but of a very *firm* grace. For God hates sin. It grieves him. Yet he can forgive it by his grace. But, as the Flood shows, you can appreciate divine grace only after you have taken divine grief seriously. Take away God's grief over sin and God's grace becomes unnecessary. So the Flood account keeps grief and grace together.

Consider, for instance, the waters of the Flood. In the ancient world water was greatly feared as a force of chaos and an agent of death. That is why Genesis 1 took pains to point out that in the creation God took the chaotic power of water and put it in its proper place. In creation God *separated* the waters from the waters and the waters from the dry land, thus carving out a safe niche for his creatures.

But the Flood was a time of uncreation as creation's barriers were temporarily lifted. Once unleashed, the waters drowned all creatures and all people outside the Ark. At the same time, however, those very same waters lifted the Ark above it all. If the Ark had not been buoyed up *by* the waters, Noah would have drowned too. The very same water that brought death to some brought life to others. Only the alchemy of God's grace could transform water from an agent of death into an agent of life. Even in the midst of the chaos of uncreation, God graciously performed an act of mini re-creation by carving out a safe niche for Noah within the ark upon the waters. God again *separated* Noah and company from the waters of death.

Likewise with the rainbow: Here again grace is active in the midst of chaos. After all, to create a rainbow, light must shine through rain. In other words, in order to show Noah a rainbow, God had to make it rain again! But this time God took the light of his grace, shined it through the rains of his grief, and so created a new symbol of hope. Indeed, as for Noah, so it has always been: God's grace appears all the more magnificent when we see it shining through the darkness of sin and its punishment of death. Grief over sin is what you would expect from a holy God. Grace is the lovely surprise — a surprise that is all the more lovely when it appears against the dark sky of sin and evil.

Princeton Seminary professor Daniel Migliore once illustrated this facet of grace brilliantly. Migliore tells of a time when he volunteered for a Vacation Bible School program in an inner-city New Jersey church. At one point during the summer they told the story of Noah. When they got to the part about the rainbow, Migliore asked, "Now, boys and girls, where do we see rainbows?" "In the street," one little boy immediately responded.

Migliore assumed that they had misunderstood the question. So he asked it again and got the same answer from a little girl. "In the street," she replied. When he checked this out with the kids, he discovered the truth: For these inner-city kids and their smog-filled environment of high-rises, the only place they ever saw a rainbow was in street puddles that had been smeared with oil. They never saw a rainbow in the sky but had seen plenty of rainbows in the greasy puddles of their burned-over urban world. But then, that is where they needed the grace of God to appear, too: Not in the sky but in the midst of the rubble and broken dreams of their day-to-day world. A rainbow "in the street" was a reminder that God's hope and grace was with them even (especially) in the squalor of the city.[1]

---

1. Daniel Migliore, "City Rainbows," in *The Princeton Seminary Bulletin* 14.1 (January 1993): 68-71.

Grief and grace are a kind of doublet in Scripture. The grief reminds us that sin is serious, that God hates it, that we need saving from it. The grief of God is properly humbling for us and perhaps a bit frightening, too. If sin is this awesome an obstacle between God and humankind, something equally awesome will have to intervene to set things right.

But this awesome sense of sin's gravity helps us fully appreciate, celebrate, and revel in the grace that saves. Only those who know just how bad sin is can also know how great grace is. For the grace of God has appeared right where you would least expect to see it: smack in the chaos of sin and evil, smack in the brokenness of our own lives. In the place where one might expect to find only grief, one sees grace as well.

And at the center of history we see a cross. That cross reminds us of God's first response to sin: grief. But just on the other side of that cross blazes the unspeakably glorious light of Easter. Just as God's grace changed the chaos of water into an agent of life, so too God has taken the ultimate chaos of sin, death itself, and has changed it into the path to life. If the cross is God's grief, the Easter light is God's grace — a light refracted through the cross as through a prism, casting the glorious rainbow of hope over all history.

CHAPTER TWO

Grace and Gratitude

SARAH, A RESPECTED church member and the mother of four, sat in the pastor's study. It was clear to Rev. Dekker that this was no social call — her inane small-talk and pressured speech clued him in that something bigger and more important was on the agenda — something that had yet to be broached. Finally, desiring to cut to the bone, the minister asked her directly, "Sarah, what brings you here today?" Then, in a burst of tears and a torrent of words, she confessed that she had had and continued to have an extramarital affair with another member of their church.

This scenario, while painful, is not uncommon. But how would we react if, in counseling further with Sarah, Rev. Dekker refused to address the rightness or the wrongness of the adultery? How would we react if his chief focus was only assuring Sarah that this sin was forgiven by Christ's grace and that nothing more needed to be said about it than that? Suppose Sarah pressed her pastor, saying, "Aren't you going to tell me this is wrong? Aren't you going to counsel me how best to stop this affair?" But suppose Rev. Dekker responded to this by saying, "No. I want you to think only about how this is forgiven by God in Christ. If I tell you it's wrong or that you should stop it, I'm afraid you'll think you are saved or damned by what you *do*. But I want you to focus only on grace. So let's forget all about this moral business and just reflect on how nothing we do, not even adultery, can separate us from the love of God that is in Christ Jesus."

Precisely this scenario, in different ways and varying forms, has been presented many times by pastor and writer Robert Farrar Capon. Few writers are better at scoring the amazingly free nature of God's grace than Capon. Few writers have more adroitly sought out, found, and destroyed the legalistic, bookkeeping Pharisee who lives in each of our hearts than Capon. Capon's reflections on grace in *The Parables of Grace* and in his other books are creative, insightful, and mostly right.

Throughout his writings, Capon's chief thesis is that in order to understand grace really and fully, we must dispense with all notions of morality. "Grace cannot prevail until law is dead . . . until morality has been bound, gagged, and stuffed unceremoniously in the trunk."[1] Capon seems convinced that to the extent that Christians maintain an interest in the shape of the moral life or in sniffing out the rightness or wrongness of any action or lifestyle, Christians evidence a deep-down desire to work their way to heaven after all, and this is nothing less than undercutting grace.

To make his point, Capon routinely shocks his readers by presenting "sin" while refusing to address it *as* sin in any traditional sense (i.e., as something that needs to be stopped, repented of, and turned around). So in his parable *From Noon to Three,* a couple gets away with an adulterous affair about which the author refuses to moralize by having the affair end or by bringing either of the persons to confess it as wrong. Capon wants the sin simply to stand on its own as a stark reminder that this, too, is forgiven by grace — even if it goes on and on and on.

More recently, in *The Mystery of Christ,* he presents a series of pastoral counseling vignettes in which he counsels a woman in adultery, a promiscuous homosexual, and others in similarly sinful situations. But in every case he steadfastly refuses to broach the morality, immorality, or sin of the activities in question lest he distract their minds from the *real* subject, namely, God's forgiveness.[2] Thus Capon counsels only that worrying about these and similar actions is pointless because, be they right or wrong, they cannot separate one from the grip of Christ's grace anyway.

1. Robert Capon, *Between Noon and Three* (San Francisco: Harper and Row, 1982), p. 7.
2. Robert Capon, *The Mystery of Christ* (Grand Rapids: Eerdmans, 1993), p. 48.

Capon at times seems essentially to say, "So what if so-called 'sin' happens? Although sin may not be a bright idea, it's no big deal in that every sin is covered by God's grace anyway. God is not in the sin-prevention business anymore; because of Jesus, God no longer takes sin seriously."[3] Capon is so convinced that moral concerns serve as a cover for a grace-wrecking works righteousness that he rebuffs nearly every concern about Christian living, every question about sin and morality, every effort to advise people on how to live for God in gratitude to Christ (though Capon does believe that some responses to God's grace are more "congruent" with grace than are others).

I mention Capon at some length because he can serve as a good introduction to the subject of this chapter — namely, once we have been saved by God's grace, then what? How do we respond to the grace of God in Christ Jesus? Capon reminds us of the two extremes with which we wrestle in this regard. On the one hand Capon does regular battle with legalists, that is, with those who dismiss God's grace in favor of keeping the rules as a way to make God love them. The legalist says, "God loves me because I'm good. As opposed to many people who lead bad lives, I'll make it to heaven because I've lived a peerlessly good life."

The opposite extreme is the one toward which Capon himself may at times tend due to the lengths to which he frequently goes to win his battles with legalists; namely, the extreme of "antinomianism," which literally means "anti-law." Antinomians are those who use grace as an excuse to live however they want, an attitude that can be summed up well in the famed words of Heinrich Heine, "God likes to forgive, I like to sin. Really, the world is admirably arranged."[4]

The twin dangers of legalism and antinomianism have from time immemorial been a kind of Scylla and Charybdis for those who write about grace. On the one hand, grace means that nothing we did in the past got us saved and that, conversely, nothing we could ever do in the future could either enhance our salvation or cut us off from it. For

---

3. Ibid., pp. 28, 191-92.

4. Of course, Capon's brand of antinomianism, if we wish to call it that, is not that extreme. Capon does not advise *that* people sin, only that they should not think God is interested in preventing them *from* sinning now that he has "solved [their] problem with sin" through Christ.

anyone who has ever fretted over his or her sin, this is good news and a very great comfort indeed.

On the other hand, however, does the availability of this all-encompassing grace mean that we can "live it up," that we can "eat, drink, and be merry" since we figure that God will forgive us anyway? Is Capon correct in stating that God is not particularly interested in whether or not we sin? If we are uncomfortable with this kind of perspective, we are still left to ponder why the good works that did us no good *before* we were saved by grace are so important to think about *after* we are saved by grace.

Author Philip Yancey once helpfully illustrated this conundrum by relating a time in his life when, as part of his graduate work, he had to study German for an entire summer in preparation for a comprehensive language exam the coming September. Since Yancey did not have a great love for the German language, and since the summer generally proffers more exciting possibilities than brushing up on umlauts and vocabulary lists, Yancey found the summer arduous and tiresome.

But he had to pass the exam and so he stuck with it. But he later wondered what his attitude would have been if someone had come to him in, say, early July, and said, "Yancey, I want you to stick with this German because it's good for you and you should put your brain to good use at all times. But I'll let you in on something. Come September, no matter how well or how poorly you perform on the exam, I guarantee you'll get a straight A."[5]

Yancey's analogy is clear: If you knew that no matter how hard you studied you would ace the exam, would you still be able to find any motivation to stick with the studying? What would prevent you from saying, "Nuts to this — I'm heading for the beach. What's the sense of studying when my grade is already in the bag?" The paradox of grace in the Christian life is actually quite similar. If grace assures us of a straight A in the kingdom of God, if the perfection of Jesus is ours already, and if every error is already covered by grace, what possible purpose could be served by our striving for goodness? Why do we not simply dispense with talking about the Christian life since the end result

5. Philip Yancey, "Why Be Good?" in *Christianity Today* 38.3 (March 7, 1994): pp. 26-29.

is "in the bag" anyway? While we may not want to go so far as to "live it up" in wanton, sinful abandon, perhaps we could at the very least dispense with worrying much about being good or living for Christ and simply take life as it comes.

In theological parlance, we are pondering the relationship between "justification" (God's forgiving us freely by grace) and "sanctification" (the process of our becoming holy). We covered justification in Chapter One — God forgives us wholly and completely by the power of grace in a once-for-all fell swoop of divine intervention through Christ. Grace is the power of God, rooted in God's abiding love, which crashes into our lives, effecting forgiveness and so making possible acceptance, revival, renewal, and reunion.

But we have also said that the power of grace does not stop at the point of forgiveness but goes on to form in us a gracious life. This is where sanctification comes in. Now sanctification can be seen in two different lights. On the one hand, it can mean being identified with the holiness of Christ. Once we are "in Christ" (Paul's favorite two-word summary for redemption), we are, as it were, "holy by association."[6]

But, more pointedly, sanctification can also be understood in the sense of a lifelong process of cooperating with the Spirit of God by the power of grace's ongoing operation. Thus already in this life we can conform ourselves more and more to the image of Christ in accordance with God's design for living. But in both senses of the word, sanctification (like the justification that preceded it) is solely and completely the work of God. Because grace is both a saving and a transforming power, we can say that even our efforts at becoming gracious are a result of grace's power and intitiative.

This point must be very clear: In both justification and sanctification God is the actor and we are the recipients of his grace. (This is vital to keep in mind. Since the Christian life is principally God's work, there is no cause to become conceited or proud of it or, as we will note below, to use it as the point of comparison between ourselves and others.)

Thus, in this chapter we must try to accomplish two tasks. First, we need to understand why, after all that has been said about grace and

6. There is obviously some overlap here with justification, by which God graciously transfers or credits Christ's righteousness to our spiritual accounts.

the uselessness of works, we still end up thinking about good works after all. What is the connection between being graced in Christ and living graciously as a result? But establishing that connection is actually the easy part, because problems crop up as soon as we return to using words like "good works" or "morality." While there is much with which to disagree in Capon's writings, at a basic level he is absolutely right: Talking about "good works" imperils the doctrine of salvation by grace alone. Since we are all legalists by nature, talking about good works may lead to trouble.

In short strokes, here is the dilemma with which we must grapple in this chapter: In order to kill legalism, we must stress the message of salvation by grace alone. But in order to avoid the happy-go-lucky life of the antinomian, we must also stress the need to *respond* to God's grace by being good and moral and Christlike. This second emphasis, however, with its stress on actions and works, can all too easily lead us *back* to the legalism that we started out trying to avoid in the first place! We cannot address the Christian life of grace without addressing good works, but we cannot address good works without putting at peril a proper conception of the grace of the Christian life!

In some ways this is similar to what a dieter goes through. On the one hand, food (or certain food, anyway) is the enemy of the waistline. On the other hand, however, even dieters have to eat some food or they will starve. So while eating food is part of an overweight person's problem, he or she still must eat even when dieting. But, as any dieter could tell you, when you are dieting, the very act of eating always carries with it the temptation to go too far and eat more than you should. The food we need to keep us alive can simultaneously be an enticement to overindulgence. So while we cannot cut out all food, it certainly would make dieting a lot easier if we could!

Similarly, Christians cannot avoid discussing good works even though broaching this subject carries with it the risk of forgetting about the grace of God. Capon's solution, to extend our diet analogy, seems to be to cut out all "food" — just stop talking about morality or good works. But this starves and malnourishes the Christian life in some important ways. So we must talk about responding appropriately to God's grace through Christlike gracious living, dangerous though this can be.

Complicating all this (as though we needed any more complications!) is the fact that, as with so much in life, these matters of legalism and antinomianism are so snarled and tangled that they can only in theory be separated into neat and distinct categories. In reality we are each of us odd admixtures of the two extremes. That is, few if any Christians are pure legalists who genuinely believe or claim that it is their morality or their Christian character that gets them to heaven.

By the same token, few if any Christians are true antinomians who go through life gleefully and willfully sinning because they agree with Heine's idea that since God likes to forgive, why not give him lots to forgive! Such pure types do not exist. Rather, most people try to stay true to the gospel of grace, but along the way they get sidetracked, tending now toward legalism, then toward antinomianism, but never, ever intending to go against the biblical witness to God's grace. Still, precisely this happens more easily and more often than we care to admit.

Attempting to strike the correct balance in this matter is dicey. Like a tightrope walker who steps out onto the air, so here we must exercise great caution and deftness, knowing that one false move, even the slightest shifting of weight to one side or the other, could bring the whole enterprise plunging into the abyss. Fortunately, the sheer fact that the subject here is grace means that there is always a divine safety net to catch us when we err and fall to one side or the other. Still, as much as possible we wish to get this right, striking the proper balance between saving grace and transforming grace. We wish to admit and recognize the paradox first articulated by the apostle James: While we are not saved *by* our actions, neither are we saved *without* them.

So we must wrestle with this desperately difficult matter. To do so we will first trace the biblical warrant for the thesis stated in the Introduction to this book; namely, that the power of God's grace not only saves but also issues in a distinctive kind of gracious living. But then, second, we will be quick to admit Capon's point that we regularly confuse this fruit of grace (the distinctive, Christlike life) with the root of our salvation (the grace of Christ). That is, we tend to view our *response* to God's grace as the *cause* of our salvation instead of being what it is, namely, the *result* of salvation. We not only "put the cart before the horse"; we turn the cart into the horse! Third, we will attempt to come up with some suggestions as to how we might strike the needed balance between graciously living the Christian life in gratitude and yet never losing sight of the utterly free, no-strings-attached nature of the grace that saves and so initiates our gratitude in the first place.

The Connection

As we noted in Chapter One, the clarion call of the Reformation was salvation by grace alone. Indeed, biblically there can be little doubt that salvation is all grace and all gift. We do not contribute to its attainment because we cannot. Our actions — both before we are touched by grace and after — cannot bring us to God. Conversely, once we are so saved, nothing we do, no sin or cluster of sins, can remove us from the grip of God's grace.

Nevertheless, there is a biblically snug fit between being saved *by* grace and subsequently living a life worthy *of* grace. Ephesians 2:8-9 is perhaps the single most frequently cited text used to substantiate the claim that "it is by grace you have been saved . . . not by works, so that no one can boast." A proper exegesis of that passage, however, cannot stop at verse 9. Ephesians 2:10 follows these ringing words of saving grace by also reminding the reader that "we are God's workmanship, created in Christ Jesus *to do good works,* which God prepared in advance for us to do" (emphasis added).

As we also noted in Chapter One, when it comes to saving grace, Paul allows no quarter for someone to say, "Grace and. . . ." Salvation is either completely by grace alone, or it is not by grace at all. Still, once salvation is accomplished by God's gracious initiative and work, the next sentence that needs to be spoken points to the life that flows *from* this grace — namely, the life of good works, of being gracious or "gracelike" as a result of being graced. "We pray . . . that you may live a life worthy of the Lord and may please him in every way: bearing fruit in every good work, growing in the knowledge of God" (Col. 1:10).

Frequently biblical scholars debate whether there is some kind of theological rift between Paul and James. Paul, after all, is so clearly the theologian of grace, while James speaks mostly of works and of the need to do something as evidence of one's faith. "You see that a person is justified by what he does and not by faith alone" (James 2:24). In that he felt there was indeed some anti-grace material in James, Martin

Luther cast a jaundiced eye on that "right strawy" epistle, even going so far as to question whether the epistle of James really belonged in the Bible.

But such a conclusion rests on a misreading of both Paul and James. While Paul is forever at pains to make clear the gracious nature of our salvation, the theological sinews that connect being graced with living graciously are everywhere to be seen. For instance, Paul speaks more than any other New Testament writer about the various gifts of the Holy Spirit. Indeed, the Greek word for "gifts" is *charismata,* which is closely related to *charis/*"grace." In fact, the various gifts that Christians receive and exercise within the church could be seen as "gracelets" or "little graces" that themselves spin out of the big Grace of Christ Jesus.

Those who receive the floodtide grace of Christ unto salvation will likewise receive many other little drippings of grace, many little "gracelets" that seep out of the overflow of that floodtide in order to help them to be productive in kingdom work. In 1 Corinthians 12, for instance, Paul takes great pains to indicate that people receive different gifts. But the underlying assumption would seem to be that *all* receive something and that all should, indeed, "eagerly desire the greater gifts" (1 Cor. 12:31). Apparently Paul saw a natural and automatic connection between being a Christian and exercising some gifts.

Paul not only speaks much about gifts but he also refers often to "fruit." However, Paul makes clear in many places that while gifts vary from person to person, the so-called "fruit of the Spirit" ought to be the goal of *all* persons. People may have fruit such as "love, joy, peace, patience, kindness, goodness, faithfulness, gentleness and self-control" (Gal. 5:22-23) to differing degrees (some people are more patient than others, for instance), but all Christians are to seek to prune away the rank fruits of evil so as to make room for and to nurture all of these good fruits of the Spirit.

In other words, when it comes to gifts of the Spirit, a person could legitimately say, "Well, I am not gifted to preach, but I do feel gifted in the area of hospitality." This is a legitimate and commonsense assertion: Not everyone is called to do or to be the same thing. But a Christian may *not* say, "Well, I am a fairly patient person, but I don't feel I have the fruit of self-control." Gifts may vary from person to person, but the fruit of the Spirit should come to all and should be sought after by all so that we might together "find out what pleases the Lord" and then do it (Eph. 5:10). The fruit of the Spirit are not like the various kinds of food in a salad bar — such that you can choose your favorites and the leave the rest off your spiritual plate — no, you must make room on your plate for them all because, for Paul, this was the only fitting way to imitate our Lord's example.

So Paul repeatedly makes clear that there is a tight linkage between grace and graciousness. The link is in fact so snug that Paul uses the radical imagery of life and death to make the point. One of the first things that grace enables is our baptism into Christ. In Paul's view, baptism is primarily a death, a participation in Jesus' crucifixion that, in turn, enables us also to share in his resurrection. What we die to, then, is sin; what we come alive to is Christ and the new life made possible by him. Thus Paul says over and again, "You died to one way of life and have come alive to a new one. Your former way of life is gone, along with all its focus on the rank fruits of evil. Your new way of life has come and with it the possibility for a new kind of garden and the bearing of a new kind of fruit. If we live by the Spirit, that is the kind of life we will pursue."

This connection between saving grace and the subsequently "gracious" life can be seen not only in specific passages but also in the broader strokes of Paul's theological brush. The great epistle to the Romans is a classic example. Having wrestled in the early chapters with sin, the Law, and the wholesale failure of human efforts to be saved by works, Paul then spends several chapters singing the doxology of God's grace ("There is therefore now no condemnation for those who are in Christ Jesus!"). But before he closes the letter, he spends four chapters dealing with the shape of the graced life. Paul covers a wide range of subjects, from the need for love and humility to the relation to civil authorities. But the overarching point is clear: Once God's glorious grace comes, everything is different. A former way of living is past (living to the body), there is a new pilot at the helm of our hearts (the Spirit), and there is a new attitude toward those around us (love).

Likewise in the epistle to the Galatians: Throughout the first portion of this letter, Paul fights tooth and nail against those who were trashing God's grace in favor of a legalistic insistence on circumcision and other such laws and human accomplishments. Paul is furious that the Galatians were beginning to view salvation as a matter of what they did or accomplished instead of what God had given in grace. Yet, before he signs off, Paul pens one of his most eloquent statements on the need to live by the Spirit, to shun the acts of the sinful nature, to bear the fruit of the Spirit, and to do good to all people. Apparently Paul saw no contradiction between insisting on salvation by grace alone and, in the same letter, insisting on a godly life of fruit-bearing and of "keep[ing] in step with the Spirit" (Gal. 5:25).

The sum of the matter comes at the very end of Galatians where Paul clearly states that the only thing that matters is "a new creation." Indeed, the idea of "newness" permeates Paul's writings. But then, why should this be surprising? As we noted in Chapter One, Paul saw grace as the single most powerful force in the universe. If it came into a person's life, how could that person fail to be changed on a fundamental level? How could one who becomes "a new creation" fail to live a distinctive life of graciousness? Any power so mighty that it could accomplish our very salvation surely would likewise transform every other aspect of life. When the divine nuclear warhead of grace detonates at ground zero in the soul, one expects the explosive effects and fallout to be far-reaching indeed.

In this sense, then, there is no conflict between Paul and James. Paul does not deny for a moment James's contention that faith will issue in good works, and that if good works are not present in any way, shape, or form, there might be good reason to doubt whether true faith was present in this person after all. James likewise would not have denied Paul's message of salvation by grace alone through faith alone; only he would have added that if a person claimed to have that kind of gracious faith while yet showing no evidence of it, that person was likely a liar. (John makes essentially the same point in 1 John 4:20a: "If anyone says, 'I love God,' yet hates his brother, he is a liar.") The power of God's grace is so enormous that it inevitably *will* result in a distinctive kind of life.

Similarly, Jesus focused a good deal of his ministry on the matter of lifestyle and obedience. As we noted earlier, everything Jesus said and did and taught is consistent with the later New Testament theological formulations on grace alone. But it is also significant that Jesus frequently enjoins his followers to obedience. In the Great Commission, one of the tasks for which the apostles are commissioned is "to teach them to obey everything I have commanded you." Likewise, as we also touched on earlier, the Sermon on the Mount radicalizes the Law of God by locating its true fulfillment in a person's heart.

Nowhere in the New Testament are we told that Jesus came to destroy the Law or to terminate its importance. Rather, he clearly said, "Do not think I have come to abolish the Law or the Prophets . . . but to fulfill them" (Matt. 5:17).[7]

So for Jesus, as for Paul and James and the other New Testament writers, once we become children of God by grace, a certain lifestyle will follow. We could sum up Jesus' attitude with his own words, "You are my friends if you do what I command" (John 15:14).

In fact, Paul's later discussion of spiritual fruit is little more than an echo of Jesus' own teaching. In Matthew's Gospel, Jesus mentions no less than 12 times the need to bear fruit. The Sermon on the Mount (recall that this was a sermon preached to those already in the kingdom) is the most clear passage on this idea. "By their fruit you will recognize them." More strongly still, Jesus states that not everyone will make it into the kingdom: "Not everyone who says to me, 'Lord, Lord,' will enter the kingdom of heaven, but only he who does the will of my Father who is in heaven" (Matt. 7:21). This facet of Jesus' teaching is also well highlighted in John's Gospel and then expanded on in John's epistles, where the need for love in imitation of Christ is stressed and repeated over and over.

John Calvin once picked up on this connection when commenting on the story of the woman who anointed Jesus' feet. Some of the people present were scandalized because a woman who was "a sinner" was touching Jesus. How could Jesus allow this? But, Calvin claimed, it should have been immediately obvious to everyone that this woman was in fact *not* a sinner, because if she had been, she would not have done a proper act of love and devotion. That her sins had already been forgiven naturally led her to a gracious act of devotion toward Jesus. The connection between grace and gratitude is so strong that merely

---

7. In Romans 10:4, Paul says that "Christ is the end of the law." But that translation fails to make clear that Paul is saying Jesus is the *telos* of the law, which means "end" in the sense of "goal" or "fulfillment" of the Law. We are told in the New Testament that Jesus came to fulfill the Law, reveal the true nature of the Law, and end the Law's stranglehold on our lives, but never does it say that the Law is "dead" because of the work of Jesus.

seeing a proper Christian life or act is itself a visible evidence of an otherwise "invisible" forgiving of sins by grace.[8]

So there is indeed a New Testament hookup between being saved by grace and subsequently living a fruitful, gracious life. Anyone who is "in Christ" is a new creation, according to Paul. This new status is most certainly *not* something we have earned or achieved; it is a gift. Still, once one is hidden away in Christ, who even now rules us as Lord from the throne of heaven; how could one fail to live a distinctive life? In general, Christians do not live for God so that God will reward them and take them to heaven someday. Rather, we Christians live for God because heaven is already there, and so, by grace, are we! "Heaven" is not merely the prize to be won at the end of history; it is also the reality to be lived today — the reality of the grace that already places us in Christ.

Although we do not have space here to elaborate further, this aspect of New Testament teaching is also a continuation of the oft-repeated Old Testament calls to holiness. "Be holy as I, the LORD your God, am holy" is the banner that flies over much of the Old Testament. Apparently nothing about the New Testament, including its radical message of God's grace in Christ, does anything to tear down that banner.

The Grateful Life

But, of course, none of this obedient imitation of Christ is done perfectly or even automatically. If we have been graced, then our tendency ought to be in the direction of gracious, godly living in obedience to Christ's command and in consistency with God's blueprint for living as found in the Scriptures. But Paul and the other New Testament writers make it clear that, for now, this will be a struggle, a battle, at times a desperately hard fight. We will not always succeed. We will not always bear the fruit of the Spirit. For such sins and failures, the grace of Christ stands ready to offer forgiveness — in fact, in a real sense those failures are forgiven even before they are committed (Capon is

8. Quoted in B. A. Gerrish, *Grace and Gratitude: The Eucharistic Theology of John Calvin* (Minneapolis: Fortress Press, 1993), pp. 92-101.

absolutely correct on that score). The grace of God is always more than a match for sin and evil.

However, the New Testament makes clear that we *should* struggle, we *should* fight, we *should* strive for the godly life of graciousness both because this is who we now are ("a new creation"), but also in gratitude to God for the gift of his grace. Conforming to the nature of Christ is "our spiritual worship" (Rom. 12:1), it redounds to God's glory (1 Pet. 2:12), and is a natural result of living in what we by grace now are, namely "righteous" (Rom. 6:13).

In the Reformed tradition, this aspect of what I am calling "the gracious life" has been called "the life of gratitude." The third and final section of The Heidelberg Catechism asks why, if we are saved by grace anyway, we still strive to do good in our lives. The answer says, in part, "[W]e do good because Christ by his Spirit is also renewing us to be like himself, so that in all our living we may show that we are *thankful* to God for all he has done for us, and so that he may be praised through us" (Question and Answer 86; emphasis mine). A major part of our being gracious is thanking God for his grace through respectfully living life the way he designed it to be lived. Such gratitude is not only a natural reaction of the graced in Christ; it is also a most *fitting* one.

But what does this emphasis on grateful living do to the message of grace and grace alone? Does a concern for morality or a pondering of what is sinful indicate a cashing out of God's grace? Not necessarily. But then, perhaps so. A short answer cannot be given in this regard because the simple, Caponesque fact is that few of us live the life of gratitude purely in the sense of grasping its proper connection to the grace that saves.

That is, by emphasizing day in and day out our need to *do* good deeds of gratitude and to *bear* the fruit of the Spirit, we can too easily begin to think only in terms of *our* actions, while God's grand action of grace fades from our consciousness. After a while, God's grace wanes and our actions wax until finally we see only what we do and forget all about what God has done. In treading the course of this vicious circle, we end up with the very legalism from which we fled in the first place.

In her modern parable "Revelation," Flannery O'Connor introduces us to Mrs. Turpin, a woman who may help us recognize some of the inherent dangers in this area of the gracious life of gratitude. As the story opens, Mrs. Turpin and her husband Claud are in a doctor's waiting room. We learn much about this woman as she surveys the others in the room. Without exception, Mrs. Turpin sizes up each person and categorizes him or her according to her own classification scheme: Some are "white trash," others are "niggers"; some are pleasant people, others are rudely quiet and ugly. As she surveys the waiting room clientele, Mrs. Turpin manages to find a categorical slot for every person there.

Indeed, we soon discover that Mrs. Turpin spends her whole life comparing herself to other people, with herself nearly always coming out better than most. Whereas some people count sheep when they are unable to fall asleep, Mrs. Turpin "counts" people instead. When unable to fall asleep, she lies in bed and pictures the mass of humanity. She then, as always, proceeds to classify each person or group by type from the bottom of the social heap to the top. Most people whom she pictures are, she believes, beneath her, although a few of the well-off and rich may be above her in the larger scheme of things. Still, she manages to view herself as better than some of even those people because she feels that she is a "good" person, whereas some rich people are not. On and on her thoughts trip until she finally drifts off to sleep, often in the end picturing the more wretched classes of people piled into a boxcar on their way to be gassed somewhere.

For Mrs. Turpin, everybody has a class or category into which he or she "fits." Usually in the end, in comparing herself to others, Mrs. Turpin feels very grateful to be who she is. In fact, she often wonders what she would do if Jesus came to her and said, "Ma'am, you can be either a nigger or a white trash, which will it be?" Although she wrestles with this, in the end she figures that she would reply, "Please, Jesus, please, just let me wait until another place is available."

But now back to the doctor's waiting room: As she sits in the waiting room with her husband, Mrs. Turpin engages another woman in conversation. In the course of their dialogue, Mrs. Turpin tips her hand and reveals the kinds of narrow attitudes with which she goes about life. Also in the waiting room is a young college girl who, after listening to Mrs. Turpin long enough, finally becomes so infuriated that she hurls her *Human Development* textbook at her and then attempts to strangle Mrs. Turpin! After they pull the girl off, she venomously spits out the words, "Go back to hell where you came from, you old wart hog." The words cut Mrs. Turpin to the quick. She cannot understand it. Granted, Mrs. Turpin thinks, a number of *other* people in that waiting room deserved to hear that kind of thing, but surely not she!

The character of Mrs. Turpin is quite pathetic and somewhat despicable. In fact, when she finally gets nailed with the girl's textbook, the reader is tempted to cheer. But Mrs. Turpin is merely bewildered by this outburst toward her because she sees herself as a genuinely good person — very kind, very giving, even to people whom she is convinced are beneath her. In fact, just before getting clobbered in the waiting room, she says, "If it's one thing I am, it's grateful." And she is. She is very grateful for her loving husband, for her life, for her religion, and for being who she is as opposed to being someone else. She views herself as a hard-working, respectable, churchgoing woman who by no means deserved to be called "a wart hog from hell." Others perhaps deserved to hear that kind of thing, but, Mrs. Turpin . . . never.

O'Connor's story powerfully reminds one of another story told once by Jesus.

"Two men went up to the temple to pray, one a Pharisee and the other a tax collector. The Pharisee stood up and prayed about himself: 'God, I thank you that I am not like other men — robbers, evildoers, adulterers — or even like this tax collector. I fast twice a week and give a tenth of all I get.'

"But the tax collector stood at a distance. He would not even look up to heaven, but beat his breast and said, 'God, have mercy on me, a sinner.'

"I tell you that this man, rather than the other, went home justified before God. For everyone who exalts himself will be humbled, and he who humbles himself will be exalted." Luke 18:10-14

A traditional "take" on this parable would be to point to the amazingness of God's grace. Like the parables of the Prodigal Son or the Laborers in the Vineyard that we considered in Chapter One, so too here the point could be made that God saves us not by what we do but by his sovereign grace alone. Further, we must die to our own efforts before we can accept the need for God's wholesale salvaging of us by grace.

Interpreted this way, this parable is yet another example of Jesus' poking holes in the self-righteousness of the Pharisees and of his opening the kingdom to the least likely of characters.

But in the context of this chapter, perhaps another viewpoint can also be advanced. Although it is easiest to regard the Pharisee in a purely negative light, perhaps we need to reconsider just who he was in his day and how he might in fact be uncomfortably similar to all of us. As many commentators have pointed out, this parable is yet another example of how Jesus designed his stories to be utterly shocking to his hearers. Parables, at least for those who first heard them, always yanked the rug out from underneath the listener's feet at the last second. The shock of landing flat on your back and staring up at the clouds was meant to jolt the hearer into rethinking conventional wisdom and past ways of thinking.

In this particular parable the shock occurred due to the high regard in which the Pharisees were held in that day. The Pharisees, though misguided in many ways, were nonetheless highly devout and therefore much respected. The form of piety that they exercised was likewise considered to be proper and fitting. In fact, some scholars have noted that even the prayer offered by the Pharisee in this parable, a prayer that we consider scandalously boastful, was a standard prayer, which had been taught to devout Jews from the days of their childhood on. In other words, this Pharisee was doing a *proper* liturgical act in offering up this prayer. No one in Jesus' original listening audience flinched or blinked at the words he said. They had heard them all before — indeed, they themselves had prayed this same prayer many times before!

The Jews of Jesus' day were taught to be grateful that they knew God, that they were not like other sinners who did not know about God and about his Law and his ways. The Pharisee, like Mrs. Turpin, was, if nothing else, grateful. But, then, so are we. We are told to be grateful to God for his salvation and to show this gratitude in all that we do. Is that wrong? Is it wrong to be thankful that we have been touched by God's grace, that we know Jesus as our Savior? Is it wrong to be grateful that we spend Sunday mornings worshiping with God's people as opposed to waking up in some crack house or sleeping off some Saturday night hangover? Is it wrong to be thankful that we are not like other people who live their lives apart from God and in disobedience to his ways?

Is the Heidelberg Catechism wrong when it lists "unchaste persons, idolaters, adulterers, thieves, drunkards, slanderers, and robbers" as "ungrateful" persons (Question and Answer 87)? Or are we, and the Catechism, essentially like the Pharisee and his "catechism"? Does our gratitude place us on a par with this Pharisee? When we (à la the Catechism) reel off a list of people we are grateful *not* to be like, is this arrogant pride? In short, what is the real, root problem of the Pharisee and of Mrs. Turpin and, just maybe, of many of us much of the time?

Perhaps the real problem is not being grateful, but being grateful only *in comparison to others*. In casting the Christian life in terms of gratitude, the question that must be asked is, "Gratitude for what and compared to what?" For the Pharisee and for Mrs. Turpin, the chief part of gratitude was that they were not like other people — that they were in fact better than most in the proudest sense.

But in reality, the only one to whom we ought to compare ourselves is Jesus Christ. Mrs. Turpin constantly wondered about Jesus coming to her and offering her options of who to become among classes and types of people whom she already despised. The more likely scenario, had Jesus ever really come to her, would have been his challenging her to compare herself only and always to himself. For the more we focus exclusively on ourselves and on our own virtues, the more likely it is that we will lose sight of the grace that saved us in the first place as well as of the ongoing grace that enables our every virtue.

Should we be grateful for being Christians as well as for the specifically Christian things we do? Yes. Paul and Jesus made clear that exercising the gifts of the Spirit and nurturing the fruit of the Spirit are chief activities of the Christian life. These are expressions of our gratitude for the gift of Christ while at the same time evidence that, as promised, the Holy Spirit is at work in us to sanctify us more and more. We are also told that we should rejoice in the fruits of our faith and give thanks for God's working in us.

In the past, especially in some strands of the Calvinist tradition, some have tried to demonstrate true spirituality by consigning all such virtues and all such fruit of the Spirit to hellfire under the guise of the statement, "All our works are as filthy rags." In his at times caustic novel *The Blood of the Lamb*, Peter De Vries recalled times when his family and minister would discuss such matters, always in the end labeling their very best virtues and deeds "filthy rags." De Vries then wryly noted, "This being our view of human merit, it can be imagined what we thought of vice."[9]

True, if we look to such works as having saving significance for us, indeed they have no merit. If we try to gain entrance into God's kingdom by offering our works to God as a kind of would-be admission ticket, they would indeed be "filthy rags." But in the context of the graced life, they are most certainly *not* filthy rags — they are graced gracelets of God's presence in our lives. Christians ought to be grateful to God for them, but we ought not to be grateful in a Turpinesque, Pharisaic way of using those things as points of comparison between ourselves and others. We should not use the fruit of the Spirit to elevate ourselves above others.

So maybe we need to be grateful for our Christian lives, but not *too* grateful. Or, better said, we need to be grateful that we can be grateful! For if we trace even our acts of gratitude back to God's gracious, sanctifying work in our hearts, we are at once put in our place. Our efforts at cooperating with the Spirit of God, while noble and necessary, are still puny compared to God's work in us. As stated above, sanctification is as much God's work as the justification that brought us into the kingdom to begin with. So we need to be concerned with fruit-bearing and the gifts of the Spirit. But when we see evidence of such things in our lives, we have no cause for boasting, no cause for pride, no cause for self-congratulation. They are, however, a cause for celebration — not a celebration of our accomplishments but of the grace that enabled them all in the first place.

C. S. Lewis once helpfully explained our situation like this: Suppose a five-year-old girl goes up to her father and says, "Daddy, can I have $5 to buy you a present?" Of course, the father gives it to her and of course the father is delighted with the gift the little girl buys for him. But it would be ridiculous to conclude that the father came out $5 ahead on the transaction![10] The only reason the little girl could buy a present is that the father gave her the money. Likewise the only reason we can do anything Christian in our lives is that God gives us the grace.

9. Peter De Vries, *The Blood of the Lamb* (New York: Penguin Books, 1961), p. 18.

10. C. S. Lewis, *Mere Christianity* (New York: Macmillan Publishing Company, 1943), p. 125.

To paraphrase Lewis again, God does not love us because we are good; he makes us good because he loves us. The roof of a greenhouse does not attract the sun because it is so bright; it is so bright because the sun shines on it.

The Pharisee in Jesus' parable and Mrs. Turpin in O'Connor's story serve as stark reminders to us that Robert Capon is right: We can all too easily confuse moral concerns with the grace that made us moral in the first place. It is frightfully easy to view the fruits of our salvation as being its roots such that we forget all about the fact that, were it not for God's initiative by grace, we would ourselves still be lost.[11]

Forgetting this basic fact by trying to live off our own merits must look ridiculous to God. For doing so inverts the whole of the Christian life such that we end up looking like a tree with its branches sunk into the earth and its roots pointing straight up into the air! Each time we try to make the evidences of God's work in our lives a point of proud comparison with others, we present just such a ludicrous spectacle. (Of course, more frightening still is the fact that a tree with its roots in the air won't live long because it will be cut off from its subterranean source of hydration and nourishment.)

In the Introduction we asserted that God's grace, while mostly a tremendous comfort, can also make life very difficult and quite complex when we try to live graciously. Here is one example of precisely this kind of "gracious complexity": Because of grace, even the grateful life can be a perilous life. It is so easy to be grateful for the wrong things. It is so easy to be grateful in the wrong way. It is so easy to use the grace-filled life to kill grace, which in turn can lead to our "killing" other people through making graceless, tactless, pathetically moralistic comparisons in our minds.

How often and how easily can this happen? Think of it this way:

11. It is ironic, as Peter De Vries pointed out, that the same Calvinists who piously *seemed* to have zero regard for their own virtues had even less regard for the vices in others. In their zest to outdo one another in pious disdain for their virtues they forgot that those virtues were themselves gifts of God's grace and, further, that without God's grace they would themselves be riddled with the very vices they disdained in others. Remembering grace might have made them properly grateful for the work of God's grace in their own lives and also properly empathetic for those who lacked such grace.

What do you think of when you spy a prostitute on a street corner or an IV drug user dying of AIDS in a hospital ward? Do you think, "Thank God for his grace! If it weren't for grace, I might have ended up like that too, and if it weren't for the further grace of God's Spirit nudging me daily into different directions, I might still end up living like that." Or do you more automatically think, "I'm certainly glad I live better than that! I'm better than those folks because I'm an up-standing member of my church and never do that kind of thing." The first perspective has the possibility of kindling empathy and compassion in our hearts for lost brothers and sisters. The second attitude leads quickly to a self-serving pat on the back. Of course, in that our Christian lifestyle is also a result of God's grace, we do need to be grateful *for* it yet without being proud *of* it. But doing that consistently is, to put it mildly, tricky.

So does that mean that we should adopt the attitude occasionally demonstrated in Capon's writings? Would we be better off mostly refusing to talk much about sin, or to engage in moral speculation, or to offer spiritual direction on the shape of the holy life? If we grant the premise that we all tend toward legalism and that we all confuse the moral life with the grace that made us moral in the first place, does that mean that we also would be better off saying that God no longer takes sin seriously and that therefore we would be better served if we focused only on the wonderfulness of forgiveness and left all thoughts on morality behind?

No, to do so would be "to throw the baby out with the bathwater." To assert that our frequent confusion is a reason not to talk about good works would be like saying (to return to our diet analogy above) that since the presence of food tempts dieters to overeat, we should do them the favor of removing all food from them. "After all," someone could claim, "since having food can make them want more food, they'd be better off not having any to begin with." Physiologically that would be ridiculous, of course — the dieter would die. But theologically it is equally ridiculous to jettison a concern for good works and a fruitful life of graciousness. As we stated above, the need to speak about good works is a deeply biblical one that we cannot dismiss just because it complicates matters for us. We may simply need to live more thought-fully and think more carefully.

In doing so we dare never forget that the central message of grace is the good news of God's forgiveness. This must always be the central focus of the life, ministry, and proclamation of the church. To return to our opening illustration: Any minister who failed to communicate the forgiveness of Christ to a troubled "Sarah" or to some other such broken counselee would be derelict in the extreme. But then, any minister who failed to take sin seriously, any pastoral guidance that failed to recognize the snug connection between being graced and living distinctively as a result, would likewise be derelict in failing to take seriously the full scope of the New Testament's words on the Christian life. Also, if we diminish sin's significance, we likewise diminish the marvelous power of God's grace, as stated in the meditation on Noah. The good news of God's grace is only really good when we first understand the enormity of sin and its ability to wound all that God has created, which, in turn, wounds God himself.

The simple, biblical fact is that sin is serious business — if it were not, surely God's Son would not have died to deal with its presence in the cosmos. In fact, as a friend of mine has noted, in the Bible it seems that creation was much easier for God to achieve than was redemption. In creation God spoke, and it was. In redemption God worked harder and longer to overcome the damage that sin wracked. The sheer nothingness of the pre-creation chaotic void appears to have been easier to overcome than the sin that later spoiled that creation.

In creation God says, "Let there be," and there is. In redemption God the Son shrieks, "My God, my God, why have you forsaken me!" and only then is there salvation. In creation God seems to take delight and leisurely pleasure in creating the universe, declaring over and again, "It is good." God even stands back on the seventh day to savor the rich diversity that sprang from his creative imagination. In redemption, however, God reduces himself to a microscopic zygote, is born, grows, sweats, suffers, weeps, and finally dies a hellish death. Only after all of that can God declare salvation accomplished and "very good."

This was so because sin and evil are a real, powerful, personal presence in the universe. Graced Christians maintain their interest in a moral life not because they wish to vitiate the good news of grace, but precisely to avoid doing that very thing. If we carelessly allowed sin a foothold in our lives or willingly went on doing that which God hates enough to die for, *that* would be the truest way to trash the truth of grace. Yes, nothing can burn grace to a cinder faster than a life of legalistic lawkeeping. But then, so to trivialize sin as to show no concern for it and hence little or no desire to eradicate it from our lives likewise demonstrates that we do not understand why *only* grace could deal with sin in the first place.

Capon claims that, yes, God takes sin deeply seriously, as evidenced by Christ's death for it. But Capon also claims that now that Christ has died and risen again, God is no longer very concerned with sin. But far too many New Testament passages point the other way. We are repeatedly warned to flee from the devil (1 Pet. 5:8-9; James 4:7; 1 Cor. 6:18; 10:14); we are enjoined to put off the sinful self and to slip on the garment of Christ (Col. 3:12-17; Rom. 13:14; Eph. 4:22-24); we are told that the Christian life is, in many ways, like a battle that we have no hope of winning unless we rely on the power of Christ and of his Spirit (2 Cor. 10:4; 1 Tim. 1:18; Eph. 6:10-18). In short, although Christ has won the victory over sin and the devil, thus giving all people the hope for and the possibility of a better life, it is not right to say that, after the resurrection, sin is treated like a nonthreatening old joke.

Sin still has the power to wound, to tear apart, to wreak havoc, and to threaten the full richness of a Christian's relationship with God. Yes, all such sins are forgiven by grace and, yes, no sin is able to remove us from the grip of God's grace. But Christians are still called to "keep in step with the Spirit," to cooperate fully with the Spirit in order to live a life worthy of grace (Col. 1:10) — a life of glorifying God with our bodies, with our talents, yes, with our very lives. In so doing we "preach" the gospel by word and by deed so that others may see and hear the good news of Jesus Christ and thus be won to his cause (1 Cor. 6:20; 1 Pet. 2:12).

Keeping Our Balance

So we come full circle to the precarious and dangerous paradox mentioned above, namely, that we are not saved by works, but neither are we saved without them. The grateful life is finally a perilous life in that we cannot live without gratitude and an earnest striving to be like Christ; yet it seems that we also have a desperately hard time not confusing the fruit of grace with the root of God's gracious working in us. We cannot be graced people without also being gracious people, but it often seems that instead of using God's gifts of grace and graciousness as a motivation to reach out to others in love, our most natural tendency is to take the gift of graciousness and turn it into a club with which to clobber others over the head. "Look how moral and good I am compared to you drug addicts, you AIDS patients, you white trash, you prostitutes! I thank you, O God, that I am not like other people!"

So how can we hope to strike the delicate balance between a legalistic insistence on living to make God love us, on the one hand, and an antinomian, "anything goes" lifestyle, on the other? How can we insist on being good and being moral without losing sight of the fact that if we succeed in these areas, that, too, adds only to God's praise and not to our own? In short, how can we focus on God's grace even in the midst of trying to be moral in response to that grace? Is it even possible to spend our days working and living for God without losing sight of God's prior working in us? Or is it inevitable that such efforts can only lead us to trash the grace of Christ?

I believe that we can engage in several spiritual disciplines to keep us focused on Christ's grace even as we work hard to thank God through our good works. Much more could be said than what follows, and even these suggestions are primarily intended to prod you into further reflection. In short, what follows is not so much a recipe for a successful spiritual balance between grace and gratitude as rough ideas to be personally appropriated and applied in life's varied situations.

The root discipline to help us in this regard is that of prayer, more specifically, of daily confession of sin within our prayers. Given the scope of the problem we have tackled in this chapter, perhaps this suggestion seems flaccid and unequal to the task. But upon reflection, we realize that an honest confession of sin might indeed achieve much in this regard. Consider: A searching, clearheaded, honest confession of sin can provide a daily self-examination as we check our souls for spiritual lumps and tumors. If we do this regularly and earnestly, we will find such spiritually cancerous lumps with great frequency and so be reminded of our need for God's forgiving grace, which, in turn, can foster daily thankfulness for it.

But including an honest daily confession of sin in our prayer regimen is neither as easy nor as automatic as it might appear at first blush. Ask yourself this question, "How often do I really confess and name my sins and shortcomings as opposed to mouthing the throwaway line, 'Forgive me, O God, for all my sins'?" Indeed, how often does any of us sift through the thoughts, words, and actions of a given day with unstinting honesty so as to discover where we crossed God's boundary lines or failed to live in the character of Christ? The simple, sad fact is that generic, generalized confession of sin is much easier and less time consuming than the real thing.

But the only confession that is worth the effort is the specific confession of nameable, targetable sins. For instance, it is only after we have recognized our pride and its specific manifestations that we can begin to seek the Spirit's help in eliminating it from our lives. We must concede before God that when we made that derogatory remark about our coworker in the lunchroom, we did so because we envied her and were trying to knock her down a few pegs. We must target our anger and realize that when we snapped at our child earlier in the day, we were in fact *not* justified for doing so but were acting out of our more selfish tendencies. We must confess not just our lusts in general, but our fantasy in bed last night of lurid goings on with the woman across from us in the office. And so on.

It is only when we can assess our lives with this kind of thorough-ness, with this kind of uncomfortable honesty, that we will have a chance to realize on a daily basis our need for God's grace. At the same time, however, this is likewise a daily opportunity for us to celebrate again the joys of grace and the reasons why the good news is good *for* us. We do not need to pretend that we are the "worst of sinners" in order to be grateful for grace. Nor do we need to work up a false sense of evil in ourselves in order to appreciate the wonders of the gospel. Rather, the simple, daily admission that we have areas of weakness, areas that are, if not ugly, certainly unattractive and in need of attention, is enough to remind us that, indeed, if salvation were up to us and our efforts, we would never make it. But then, neither do we need to make it on our own: Another has already done his best for us, and that is more than enough.

It may be distressing and depressing to sift through an average day, realizing that here and there we were really rather nasty. But that depression and sense of distress are nothing compared to the relief we can feel when we realize again that all of that, and all of the other sins that we cannot even recall specifically, are already forgiven by the grace of Christ. The murmuring sigh of relief that we exhale when someone rubs a sore spot on our back just right is exactly the kind of joyous exhalation we should experience at the end of every prayer we utter.

Even the last words of the Christian's prayer — the words "For Jesus' sake . . ." — remind us that it is for the sake of Jesus and his grace that I am able to make this prayer and confess these sins. It is for his sake and because of his grace that I do all of these activities and receive all of this forgiveness. That is a joyous reminder, indeed, and one that can and ought to serve as a daily knock between the eyes for any of us who are tempted to become proud or stuffy by comparing ourselves to others.

A second idea, closely related to this, is to foster in ourselves an abiding humility. The deadly sin of pride has traditionally been regarded as the root sin of the human race. If that is so, it may likewise be true that humility (pride's antidote) is the root virtue of the Christian life. In his book *Spirituality and Human Emotion,* Robert C. Roberts called humility the chief "moral project" upon which to build the rest of our spirituality.[12]

Roberts also points out that, contrary to popular opinion, humility does not mean regarding yourself as lower than all other people, as being the worst of the worse. Humility does not mean having unhealthy self-esteem. Rather, humility, properly understood, is that virtue by which we view all people as being essentially equal. I am neither better nor worse than other persons. Just because I can do action "X" better than someone else does not mean that I *am* superior but only that I have a gift the other person lacks. But then, he no doubt has talents in areas where I am not gifted. Only sinful pride would dupe me into believing that the areas in which I am gifted are more important than the areas in which others are gifted. So, for instance, a preacher should never assume that his or her gifts in the pulpit are more important than the gifts a gentle hostess demonstrates around her dining table. Likewise, the gentle hostess should never assume that her area of giftedness is automatically more important than the area of music in which another person might be talented.

Humility means seeing life as an essentially level playing field. When all the pluses and minuses of people are taken into account, we all come

12. Robert C. Roberts, *Spirituality and Human Emotion* (Grand Rapids: Eerdmans, 1982), pp. 57-73.

out the same before God. We all need God's grace (ultimately and daily), and that same grace gives all of us various gifts (albeit in differing areas and perhaps to differing degrees). Given that, we should base our self-assessments not on comparisons with others but simply on the fact that God loves us in Jesus Christ. (In the next chapter we will need to consider the difficulties of doing this in a peculiarly capitalistic society where rewards, punishments, and competition are a way of life.) If we can foster humility through daily meditation on God's grandeur, and if this is then dovetailed with a keen awareness of our own sinfulness, perhaps we can deflate our pride. If so, we will have gone a long way toward keeping ourselves from the unhealthy comparisons by which we twist the gracious life of gratitude into an ungracious life of one-upmanship.

A third kind of discipline in which we can engage to help keep our gracious balance in life comes from, of all people, the atheistic philosopher Friedrich Nietzsche. By considering some of his thought, we may find a more healthy way to think about even the Christian virtues we work so hard to cultivate. Among other claims, Nietzsche asserted that all humility, especially among Christians, is essentially "a will to power," a ploy by which to elevate ourselves above others after all. Nietzsche was convinced that actions are never what they appear to be and that even the most altruistic of actions may very well be fueled and motivated by a desire for fame or power or some such less-than-admirable motive.

In the past Nietzsche has been anathematized by Christians because of his atheistic bent and his vicious attacks on Christianity. (Nietzsche's reputation has also been sullied through the association of his thought with the later development of Nazi ideology.) But in *Suspicion and Faith,* philosopher Merold Westphal claims that there may be much that we Christians can learn from Nietzsche. Westphal claims that Nietzsche, Sigmund Freud, and Karl Marx were "atheists of suspicion"; that is, they disbelieved in God primarily because they were highly suspicious of the motives that lay behind people's believing in Christianity in the first place. They did not have theoretical, philosophical arguments against the existence of God; rather, they believed that Christians themselves were perpetuating a myth in order to advance less admirable desires, wishes, or plans.[13]

13. Merold Westphal, *Suspicion and Faith: The Religious Uses of Atheism* (Grand Rapids: Eerdmans, 1993).

One of the chief reasons why Nietzsche regarded Christians with wariness was that he suspected that something less than pure, less than holy, less than genuine stood behind Christian efforts at humility, love, compassion, and the like. As Westphal says, when Nietzsche regarded some Christian virtue, he always looked at it squintingly. Rather than accept a given act of altruism at face value, Nietzsche narrowed his eyes and asked, "*Why* did you just do what you did?" Nietzsche's own suspicion was always that a will to power was behind a given act of humility or some such moral virtue. So, to use an admittedly extreme example, were Nietzsche still alive today, he would squintingly behold Mother Teresa and ask, "Why is she doing all that work with the lepers of Calcutta? Somewhere hidden behind her gentle, saintly facade there must be a deep-down desire for fame and fortune that is driving her to do this work and so get all this attention. She's not humbly self-effacing at all — it's all an act!"

It is not our purpose here to enter into a deep dissection of Nietzsche's thought. At minimum we would recognize that the extremes to which Nietzsche's rhetoric and suspicions go are absurd and so are often patently false. Still, as Westphal points out, we can recognize something right about what Nietzsche alleged, something that may even prove helpful to us in going about our daily self-checkups through a confession of sin. This is so because, as Nietzsche properly pointed out, right acts are hollow if they are done for the wrong reasons.

Take a very common example: If a child in a nursery takes one of her crackers and offers it to a child who has none, there is something lovely about the action. Whatever his or her exact motivations, most would smile over a proper act of apparent love and altruism. But suppose a mother came up to her son, asked him to share a cracker with a little girl without any, only to have the boy burst into angry tears punctuated with shouted protests of "No!" If the little boy did finally stomp over to the little girl and tearfully shoved the cracker over to her with a sneering, "Here!" well, we would be less than impressed. It would be the same action of sharing in both situations and with the same result: The child without a cracker would end up having one to eat. But the radically different attitude and motive of the second child would, to say the least, temper our approval of the action. In fact, we might even be tempted to say, "The kid could better have kept his lousy cracker if that was how he was going to give it to the poor little girl!"

Such is the nature of Nietzsche's critique of Christian virtue. The sad fact is that it is distressingly easy to do the right thing but for very wrong reasons. These "glittering vices" do not accrue to our moral credit for the same reason that we would not laud the act of sharing by the pouting child in the nursery. So perhaps we might pat ourselves on the back for *not* engaging in a certain activity — perhaps we resisted making a pass at our attractive coworker, for instance. But who is to say that the real reason for our failing to flirt was not a desire to live in God's pattern for sexuality but rather sheer cowardice? Maybe the reason we did not slip her a glance or put our arm around his shoulder sprang more from a fear of getting caught or being spurned than from a deep desire to show gratitude to God for the salvation graciously given to us in Christ!

The same could be alleged for proper actions that we do perform. Perhaps we gave the money to the charity, went to the church service, or volunteered an hour of time at the homeless shelter. How do we know that these good actions sprang from right motives? Perhaps we were trying to enhance our standing in the community, or maybe we feared that God was keeping track of our good and bad deeds on some cosmic tote board. Maybe we picture God as some grand Santa Claus who knows whether we have been "naughty or nice," and we would just as soon keep our tally of good deeds ahead of our bad. How can we be certain that, at the very least, we were not acting out of a mixed bag of motives, some pure but others sullied by self-serving interests and desires?

The more we reflect on the limitless possibilities for human self-deception, the more we realize that, even at our best, we can simultaneously be at our worst. None of this is to claim that Christians *never* act for God out of pure motives, but only that it is hard to be *certain* that we are doing so and that, in truth, many times our motives are less than spiritually pure. I have always found it frightening to wonder how many unholy activities I might try if someone (some demon?) would give me the assurance, "You won't ever get caught!" The sheer fright that that prospect gives may itself be an indication that all too often it is more social opprobrium and less spiritual holiness that causes me to act or to refrain from acting in the moral realm.

When examining the moral life of which we are often so proud and for which we are so grateful, we would do well to pray with the squinted eyes of Nietzsche. Just what *is* motivating our actions? How do we know that we have done the right thing for the right reason? Many times we are not even sure. The bottom line is that the Christian life is a lifelong process not only of becoming more Christlike but also of becoming more Christlike in the right way and for the right reasons. These are concurrent and parallel struggles the presence of which serves as a grim reminder of the frightful complexity of the human heart in sin.[14]

But this also reminds us that while we need to be grateful for our Christian lives and while we should thank the Holy Spirit for working in us, that life of gratitude should never be the point of comparison between ourselves and others. Even the most outwardly glittering Christian life is frequently flawed and in need of grace to repair its shortcomings and forgive its less-than-pure motivations. Remembering this will keep us so busy relying on God's daily grace that we will not have the time or energy left to compare ourselves proudly to others. As we stated above, the only one we need to be better than is Jesus himself. A healthy assessment of how we are doing on that score will always drive us to our knees in confession.

In the end, we must be grateful to God above all for the grace that saved us. We can express that gratitude in a number of ways, such as through earnest moral striving to be conformed to the image of Christ in obedience to all that God commands. Ironically, however, we need to be grateful also for being able so to express our gratitude! That is, we are grateful for the Spirit's enabling us to be grateful!

Summary

To receive the enormous gift of God's grace means responding in gratitude with a gracious life in which we exercise our spiritual gifts, bear clusters and clusters of rich spiritual fruit, and pursue good works that redound to God's glory and thus provide a vivid witness to the faith, hope, and new life that are in us. We have wrestled in this chapter

---

14. The meditation on Samson following Chapter Three will highlight how we are all a mixture of light and darkness and that, many times, we live in the shadowed border areas where the darkness leaves off and the light begins.

with striking the proper balance between remembering and celebrating God's grace while at the same time doing deeds of grace and gratitude in return. The dilemma we have tried to solve springs from the fact that although the Christian life is finally all about *receiving* God's grace, it also must include much *doing* of God's will.

But as Robert Capon reminds us, our most natural tendency is to confuse the doing with the receiving; that is, we forget that we can only be gracious because we first received grace. In this sense, then, we need to remember that the difference between ourselves as Christians and those who are not Christians is *not* that we live morally whereas they do not, for that is a surface comparison only, not one of inner depths. Such thoughts can only lead to proud comparisons and legalistic nitpicking. The only difference between a Christian and a non-Christian is that the Christian received God's grace as a gift. But since it is ridiculous to feel proud of a gift, we are led to a more tender and compassionate perspective on those around us and a more humble, grateful perspective on ourselves.

In order to help keep our perspectives in plumb on these deep and difficult subjects, we also suggested that a rigorous life of prayer and self-examination may help foster both an awareness of our own sin and gratitude for the grace that forgives that sin every day. We also suggested a Nietzschean "squinting" at our own moral deeds and virtues in order to realize that, while such "fruits" are themselves a result of God's grace, they often remain imperfect even at that. A healthy suspicion of our own motives may be one step we can take to keep ourselves from using the result of God's grace as a way to forget about God's grace.

After all, if we can recognize an occasionally sinful motivation behind even the good we do, we will be much less quick to use those good things as a point of comparison in that we will, once again, be impelled back to grace and grace alone. Christians should be so busy reflecting on and giving thanks for grace that no time will be left for proud appraisals of the grateful lives we attempt to lead.

When the apostle John wrote that "we have received grace upon grace," out of the fullness that is Christ (John 1:16, RSV), perhaps he meant in part that grace never stops. We noted earlier that sanctification (the process of becoming holy in our day-to-day living) is as much the gracious work of God as was the justification that began the entire process. Indeed, we never stop needing or receiving the grace of God. Grace granted us faith, forgave us our sins, placed us "in Christ," and now continues to enable our every virtue and forgive our every failure — yes, even the failures that take place smack in the midst of our virtues! It is this perspective that can help keep us humble, even in the midst of our busy lives of gratitude.

Jesus said, "Whoever exalts himself will be humbled, and whoever humbles himself will be exalted" (Matt. 23:12). At the end of the story "Revelation," Mrs. Turpin has a "revelation" of precisely this kind. Having entertained in her mind many revelation-scenarios of Jesus' coming to her, Mrs. Turpin finally does really meet Jesus. (Mrs. Turpin was literally "touched by grace" in this story since the college girl in the waiting room was named Mary *Grace*!) But as you might expect, the picture is very different.

For Mrs. Turpin sees in her mind's eye a ladder going up to heaven. On it are gathered the lot of humanity — the same group that Mrs. Turpin often pictured in boxcars on their way to be gassed. But in this dream they are all treading the heavenward way, with the *bottom* of Mrs. Turpin's social scale leading the way and with Mrs. Turpin and her kind taking up the rear. As she observes this picture, Mrs. Turpin can see her very virtues burning off like the morning dew — the very virtues for which she was so grateful and by which she had elevated herself above others. What she is left with is nothing but grace and grace alone. Flannery O'Connor does not tell the reader just how Mrs. Turpin reacted to this final "revelation." But one hopes that she still felt, well, *grateful!*

MEDITATION

The Wound of Grace

GENESIS 25–33

JACOB WAS A CROOK. The Bible does nothing to hide this fact from us even though Sunday school versions of him softpedal his true nature. But, as we will see, while Jacob was a crook, at least he was *God's* crook. For in the story of Jacob, we see the irony of God's being active in the life of a schemer. But through this irony, and only through it, we can learn something about the nature of grace.

Before Jacob is born, the biblical text reminds us, God is sovereign as he works out his ancient promise to Abraham. As with Abraham and Sarah a generation earlier, Isaac and his wife Rebekah also face the tragedy of barrenness. So they pray to God, and only then does Rebekah conceive. But why did God repeatedly choose barren women to help make his mighty nation as numerous as the stars in the sky? Why not choose women who were fertile in the first place? Perhaps because God wanted to remind everyone that he was in charge. God, and God alone, was the one who would move his promise along in history.

God further shows his sovereign control over the life of the promise by a shocking reversal of social convention. God comes to Rebekah and tells her, "You've got twins within you. But I will make the younger of the two the greater." This was shocking in the biblical world in that the practice of primogeniture, favoring the oldest child, was very ancient. For God to come and reverse this custom was radical. But again, God shows that if his promise is kept and a mighty nation is forged, it will not be because of human will or human practices or human achievement. God's people will be a people of grace.

79

So just before Jacob makes his appearance on the biblical stage, God sets that stage by placing his grace right up front. But it would be many years before Jacob learned about grace. For Jacob is a man of conflict — a scrappy schemer who gets ahead by his wits and cleverness. Already at his birth Jacob comes out of the womb with his little hand grabbing the heel of his brother Esau. So they name him *Jacob* or "Heel-Grasper" — a name that carried with it a definite ring of deception, cleverness, and one-upmanship. Jacob would forever be pushing someone back or down so as to propel himself forward or up.

The rest of Jacob's life will bear out the appropriateness of his name. Whether he was swindling Esau out of his inheritance, blatantly swiping his father's blessing, or cheating his Uncle Laban out of most of his wealth, Jacob was a man who lived by his wits.

Along the way, however, God occasionally reminds Jacob of his presence. When fleeing the fury of his brother Esau, for instance, Jacob has a dream of a ladder going to heaven with God at the top, Jacob at the bottom, and the angels ascending and descending between. In this dream, God, by his grace, promises Jacob life, land, and fruitfulness. When Jacob awakes, he is very thankful — it sounds like a pretty good deal to him. Still, he hedges his bet by saying, "OK, God, *if* you do all that you say you'll do, then I'll be a believer." Instead of reveling in God's grace, Jacob transmutes the dream into a kind of business deal. Jacob then picks himself up and makes his way to his Uncle Laban's ranch for many more years of grabbing, grasping, and grappling.

Indeed, it will be a number of years before Jacob learns the wonder of grace finally and fully. Many years after his dream, on the eve of meeting his brother Esau once more, Jacob is very busy preparing for the encounter. Jacob plies all his skill to plot the best strategy to avert disaster in the event that Esau still held a grudge. But on the eve of this planned meeting, Jacob has an unplanned encounter. Alone on the banks of the Jabbok River, Jacob wrestles all night with an unknown assailant. As they kick and grapple, Jacob realizes that whoever this assailant is, he is very strong. But Jacob is as scrappy as they come, and so he manages to keep from getting licked.

But then, just before dawn, the Stranger reaches down, merely touches Jacob's hip, and instantly dislocates it. Then the Stranger asks to be released. By now Jacob has sensed that this may be someone special. So he wipes the mud from his mouth and begs for a blessing.

What he gets instead is a new name. "No longer will you be 'Heel-Grasper,' struggling with people and getting ahead by your wits. From here on out you will be 'Israel' — the one who wrestles with God and gets ahead only by God's blessing." Then the Stranger blesses Jacob after all and disappears. Jacob realizes that he has seen and wrestled with God face to face, and so he calls this spot "Peniel," meaning "the face of God."

At last Jacob's life is changed. In the most important encounter of his life, he realizes that his wits and deviousness did him no good. All night long he thought that he could get the best of this fellow the same way he had gotten the best of Isaac, Esau, and Laban. But when it was all over, Jacob was beaten with a mere brush of the divine hand; only then was he blessed.

Frederick Buechner has famously called this "The Magnificent Defeat." For it was the end of Jacob's scheming and relying on his own wits. All his life Jacob had grabbed for and then successfully snagged various blessings. But when it came to getting the greatest blessing ever — God's blessing — he had to be defeated in order to realize that the greatest thing in life comes only by grace. But the grace wounded him, too. The limp he would have for the rest of his days would remind him of grace and its power. Indeed, Jacob learned that the greatest power in the universe is not clever wits or rippling muscles. No, the most stunning power is that of grace.

In fact, in Genesis 33, when Jacob and Esau finally meet again, it is clear that Esau has long forgiven Jacob and is only too happy to see him again. Jacob is bowled over by this favor and so he blurts out in verse 10, "To see your face is like seeing the face of God." This is not the voice of old, crooked Jacob. This is the voice of Israel. For Jacob had seen firsthand the gracious face of God and now, amazingly, he felt something of that same forgiving grace reflected in Esau's gap-toothed smile. Jacob finally knew that the most important thing in life was seeing just that face of grace. Nothing else mattered now.

One of the last portraits the Bible gives us of Jacob comes from Genesis 48, where Jacob's son Joseph brings his two sons for Jacob to bless. At the last second, however, Jacob crosses his hands and gives the greater blessing to the younger boy. Joseph tries to stop him, "Dad, you're confused. You've got to place your right hand on the older boy." But Jacob was not confused. He knew that being firstborn, being stronger, being more clever, did not get a person "in" with God. To get in with God takes grace, and in the last action of his life, by crossing his hands, Jacob shows how much he had learned about that.

But it is a hard lesson, this lesson of grace — a hard and deeply wounding lesson. (Even Mrs. Turpin had to be wounded by Mary Grace before she had her revelation.) We would all just as soon try to make it on our own. In fact, whether we admit it or not, we often do think we are making it on our own. We so easily forget grace. We so easily make as the point of comparison between ourselves and others not the grace that saves but our own moral strengths. But it is precisely those strengths that the grace of God wounds. God sends our best hobbling off to the horizon as a reminder that, when it comes to salvation, those things do us no good.

As Buechner so memorably reminds us, Jacob limping away against the dawn sky at Jabbok reminds us of Another who hobbled away from an empty tomb on pierced feet, limping against the glorious conflagration of the Easter dawn. In the holes that marred his hands, his feet, and his side we see the defeat of human effort. If that is what it takes to be saved, we do not have what it takes. We must stop trying. We are done in. Defeated. But this is a magnificent defeat, for it opens us to receive grace and its life-giving victory. Blessed are they who limp, for they shall walk with Jacob and with Jesus into the kingdom of God.

CHAPTER THREE

Grace and Capitalism

Now a man came up to Jesus and asked, "Teacher, what good thing must I do to get eternal life?"

"Why do you ask me about what is good?" Jesus replied. "There is only One who is good. If you want to enter life, obey the commandments."

"Which ones?" the man inquired.

Jesus replied, " 'Do not murder, do not commit adultery, do not steal, do not give false testimony, honor your father and your mother,' and 'love your neighbor as yourself.' "

"All these I have kept," the young man said. "What do I still lack?"

Jesus answered, "If you want to be perfect, go, sell your possessions and give to the poor, and you will have treasure in heaven. Then come, follow me."

When the young man heard this, he went away sad, because he had great wealth.

Then Jesus said to the disciples, "I tell you the truth, it is hard for a rich man to enter the kingdom of heaven. Again I tell you, it is easier for a camel to go through the eye of a needle than for a rich man to enter the kingdom of God."

When the disciples heard this, they were greatly astonished and asked, "Who then can be saved?"

Jesus looked at them and said, "With man this is impossible, but with God all things are possible." (Matt. 19:16-26)

IF YOU ASKED the average Christian the meaning of this well-known incident, the answer would likely go something like this: "Well, this man loved his money more than he loved God. For rich people, it's hard to be saved because it means giving away what they prize most highly, namely, their wealth. Jesus asked this man to do just one thing to be saved, but he couldn't do it because he just didn't love God as much as his money."

But is the love of money the core problem here? Granted that the love of money is "the root of all evil." Granted that greed, or "avarice" (which is one of the "Seven Deadly Sins"), can impede a person's relationship with God. But is that the Rich Young Man's primary problem?

No, it appears that something else is going on here that may point to a problem much closer to home for most of us, irrespective of how much money we have deposited in the bank. What Jesus seems to be getting at in this acted-out parable is that a can-do, work-your-way-to-heaven attitude blocks grace. "Teacher, what good thing must I *do* to inherit eternal life?" It was the wrong question. Long before one discovers this man's inability to part with his money, he should discover what Jesus detected: a fundamentally wrongheaded approach to salvation. As we noted above, the tenor of Jesus' entire ministry is that it is not what you do or fail to do that includes you in or excludes you from God's kingdom. Rather, it is God's initiative in grace that saves. The Rich Young Man's problem was that he viewed salvation as a business transaction — you work for God, he pays you a wage in the currency of salvation.

It is curious to note that Matthew's Gospel is the only one of the Synoptic Gospels that has the man asking Jesus, "What *good* thing must I do?" Mark and Luke have him saying, "*Good* teacher, what must I do. . . ." Given Matthew's Jewish reading audience and his interest in deflating self-righteousness so as to inflate God's grace, this may be a significant variation. For the phrase "good thing" clues the reader in that this incident, like similar run-ins with the Pharisees, is finally all about good works versus God's free grace. This man knew that goodness was involved in salvation, but he seemed to think that the goodness had to begin on the human side, with God doing little more than responding in kind with some type of reward.

Jesus' reply shows his immediate incredulity toward the man's approach. "Why do you ask me about what is good?" In other words, "Why are you even thinking about what *you* can do? There is only One who is good, and you are not he." Jesus' subsequent listing of commandments may seem to be a validation of the Young Man's approach, as though Jesus were saying, "Well, let's see . . . what good thing *should* you do? Well, try these laws on for size." I believe, however, that Jesus is using irony to show the man how foolish his approach really was. Jesus reels off an impossible list of demands (impossible for sinners, that is) as a way to show the man that if it is working his way to heaven that he wants, he will never make it. This exchange is a little like that of a man with two fractured legs asking someone, "What must I do to make you love me?" and then being told, "Run around the block right now!" Jesus was *refuting* the Young Man's approach, not playing into it.

Although the other Gospels tell us that Jesus "loved" this man (and I do not doubt he did), I still picture Jesus as frowning in frustration when the Young Man responds to Jesus with the surprising words, "All these have I kept!" So then Jesus falls back, regroups, and goes for this man's weakness. By telling him to sell all that he had, Jesus was not establishing a rule for all Christians in all times. Nowhere does the Bible tell us to sell everything and give to the poor, and Jesus is not making that a rule here, either. Rather, he is going for the chink in this man's armor.

True, Jesus could have gone back to his material on the Sermon on the Mount and said, "Really? All those you have kept since your youth? You've never lusted in your heart? You've never called your brother a dirty name?" But Jesus does not do that. Instead he recommends something that he senses this man would have a hard time doing. Jesus does this as a way to show him that no matter how perfect he thinks his life is, no matter how peerlessly he has kept the Law (and this man probably was a very devout, earnest man — his self-deception aside), if he wanted to work his way to God, he would always fall at least a little bit short — if you want to make salvation into a game or competition, you have to accept the consequence, namely, you must be perfect to win. For if salvation is a game, then "close" is not only not good enough, it is positively hell.

So the core problem for the Rich Young Man was *not* that he loved money more than God. His problem was that he approached all of life as if it were a business deal. His problem was a kind of can-do spirit that viewed all of life as reward or punishment based on merit and effort alone. If it really is "hard" for a rich person to enter God's kingdom, it is not only the love of money that brings difficulty, but rather the self-reliant, can-do attitude that frequently characterizes the rich. After all, in Jesus' day as in our own, to get ahead in life requires great cleverness, savvy, and hard work (think of Jacob in the meditation above). After spending a lifetime relying on his or her own strength and brainpower to get ahead, such a person finds it difficult to admit wholesale weakness, failure, and sin. As it was for Jacob, so this Rich Young Man was wounded by his encounter with God and his grace. He, too, hobbles off toward the horizon at the end of the story.

It is hard for the self-reliant to rely on God's grace alone for life's ultimate good: eternal life. It is not that the camel *cannot* go through the eye of the needle; it is just that the *camel* cannot do it — only God can pull him through. "With man this is impossible, but with God all things are possible." Some commentators think that "the needle" to which Jesus refers is The Needle Gate in Jerusalem, which was a particularly small, narrow gate through which a camel would indeed have a hard time passing. But I think it better to take Jesus' metaphor head-on and think about a sewing needle and a double-humped Arabian camel. If we seek ways to cash out the metaphor's radicalness, we still allow the possibility of the camel squeezing through on its own, and that is not Jesus' point at all.

This interpretation of the Rich Young Man's problem is confirmed by this story's placement in Matthew. Just prior to this incident, Jesus had taken the little children to himself and recommended their humility, their nonstatus in life as being the kind of attitude needed to enter God's kingdom. In Jesus' day, children were viewed as losers, almost as being not quite human. Childhood was not looked at as the charming, innocent time of life that we see it as today. Rather, childhood was viewed as something to be beaten out of a child as soon as possible so that he or she could become a real person, that is, an adult.[1]

By recommending that all true disciples be like these little ones, Jesus was (shockingly) holding up powerlessness as a model to follow. "Be like these little ones who are not proud, who can do nothing in life, but who still can receive the greatest gift of all by grace alone."

1. See Robert Farrar Capon, *The Parables of Grace* (Grand Rapids: Eerdmans, 1988), p. 17.

Because this incident comes immediately before the Rich Young Man appears on the scene, these children are likely a kind of dramatic foil to him. He was the very antithesis to life's losers. He was a winner — a powerful man for whom no transaction was too difficult. He was a wheeler and dealer, and it showed.

But notice, too, that immediately following this incident Jesus tells the Parable of the Laborers in the Vineyard. As we noted in Chapter One, this parable overturns good economic sense and undercuts the merits of human effort by making clear that God gives grace away to everyone, regardless of effort or deserving. The incident with the children and this parable frame the Rich Young Man's story, thus placing it within the larger gospel theme that grace means that we do not "win" by our own striving.

We have examined this incident because, as we will try to show in this chapter, the Rich Young Man and his attitudes toward life and salvation have some clear implications and resonances for today. For, as we will explore, we Americans live in history's single most powerful "can-do" culture ever. Ours is the culture of capitalism — of the "American Dream," of rags-to-riches stories, and of "pulling yourself up by your own bootstraps." What is more, this capitalistic spirit is heralded as the best approach to culture and commerce ever developed.

Why Do We Need to Think about This?

Among those who promote democratic capitalism as the best way to secure human liberty and human happiness (economically at least) and bring peace to society are a large number of Christian theologians. Michael Novak claims that "Under democratic capitalism, the individual is freer than under any other political economy ever experienced by the human race."[2] Likewise Peter Berger feels that "Capitalism, through its sheer ability to deliver the goods, has emerged as the most revolutionary force in human history."[3] Richard John Neuhaus recently

2. Michael Novak, *The Spirit of Democratic Capitalism* (New York: Simon and Schuster, 1982), p. 339.

3. Peter Berger, ed., *The Capitalist Spirit: Toward a Religious Ethic of Wealth Creation* (San Francisco: Institute for Contemporary Studies), p. vii.

observed that, in his opinion, "capitalism is the economic corollary of the Christian understanding of human nature and destiny."[4] Even Pope John Paul II, in his 1991 encyclical *Centesimus Annus,* approved of the free market and of capitalism (properly defined) as "the most efficient instrument for utilizing resources and effectively responding to needs."[5]

In this chapter I do not intend to critique or assess the capitalist business system from a Christian point of view, nor do I intend to present any alternative economic system as being more or less Christian than the current capitalist one. Much ink is spilled these days debating and pondering the relative justice and ethics of capitalism, of seeking after profits, and related economic themes. But again, creating an ethics of business or investigating the justice of capitalism and its relationship to the poor of the earth will not be my focus here. Although I am wary of theologians who "baptize" capitalism or any given system as being a truly Christian economy, democratic capitalism may well be an excellent system of producing and distributing economic goods and services. The freedoms and opportunities presented in a free market economy may accord well with human dignity and responsibility. But debating the ins and outs of that will not be my purpose in this chapter.

Furthermore, Christians do have a right and a responsibility to be involved in commerce. Likewise, thoughtful theologians have an equal responsibility to ponder in a Christian way the meaning of it all. The "cultural mandate" of Genesis 1 (the charge by God to rule the earth on his behalf) means that we have a responsibility for stewardly management of all the gifts and goods God has given us — including economic ones. Christians, therefore, have the right and the responsibility to be involved in business. Nothing I say in what follows is meant to undermine this fundamental perspective. Although, as we will note below, Christian businesspersons may want to alter some of their views and practices so as to accord better with a biblical understanding of the life of grace, Christians in business should not be made to feel that their occupation in the world of American capitalism is itself

4. Richard John Neuhaus, *Doing Good and Doing Well* (New York: Doubleday, 1992), p. 184.

5. *Centesimus Annus* ¶¶34-35, quoted in Neuhaus, *Doing Good and Doing Well,* p. 296.

sub-Christian, unspiritual, or any more hazardous to their faith than other "can-do" vocations.

So I am not attempting to write a treatise on business ethics, capitalist justice, or the proper Christian view of economics. Rather, the goal of this chapter is a more modest one (though not for that reason any less important): We need to ask, "What effect has the capitalist way of life had on the church, its theology, and, most important, its view of grace?" Can people who inhale the air of democratic capitalism exhale the air of grace in Christ? Can people (like the Rich Young Man) who spend most of life thinking in terms of earnings and savings and self-reliance step out of that in their churches, homes, and families so as to incarnate the fundamental grace that forms the gospel's core element?

These are vital questions for Christians to consider. For the simple fact is that capitalism is more than a way of business — it is a pervasive cultural ethos. President Calvin Coolidge is reported to have said, "The business of America is business." And so it is. As Michael Novak adroitly points out, "Democratic capitalism is not just a system but a way of life. Its ethos includes . . . a new and distinctive conception of community, the individual, and the family."[6]

Of course, many of the issues involved in this ethos are not particularly new or unique to capitalism. As the Parable of the Laborers in the Vineyard makes clear, having a sense of earning rewards and getting only what you deserve has been true of people throughout the span of history. The Old Testament is itself replete with words of advice to shopkeepers, vendors of goods, and the like. Full-blown democratic capitalism may be a comparatively recent economic innovation, but many of its salient attitudes are not of recent manufacture.

Still, there is something unique about the capitalist spirit — something that was not true until fairly recently. As Rich DeVos points out in his book *Compassionate Capitalism,* it was only after the publication of Adam Smith's *The Wealth of Nations* that the individual became paramount. "Up until this time, people hadn't always thought of themselves as individual agents, free to make decisions on their own. They thought of themselves as members of a community or class. With the old way of thinking, decisions were made by consensus or fiat, and the

6. Novak, *The Spirit of Democratic Capitalism,* p. 29.

individual didn't count for much."[7] Now, however, (as evidenced by DeVos's own writing) the individual is clearly more in focus. DeVos himself keys on the individual by telling him or her, "Say to yourself, 'I'm not a loser, I can and I will succeed.' You can do it!"[8]

The focus on the individual entrepreneur, the sense that we must take responsibility for ourselves, the "can-do" spirit that leads to the much celebrated "rags-to-riches" stories in which Americans revel — all of these developments are comparatively recent and spin mostly out of the capitalist ethos. So while we will be dealing with themes that transcend capitalism, we must recognize that most of the items discussed below are magnified and highlighted by democratic capitalism in ways seldom before seen in history.

But, of course, readers familiar with the rise of capitalism may already have perceived another wrinkle: the very Protestant Reformation that taught salvation by grace alone also aided and abetted the rise of the capitalist spirit. The Reformation teachings on work, the holiness of every vocation, and especially John Calvin's well-known writing on the practice of usury all conspired in some way to legitimize the seeking of profits and the opening of the markets to trade and free commerce.[9]

Even the modern capitalist focus on the individual has some Reformation roots. As Charles Taylor noted in his sweeping study *Sources of the Self,* the Reformation idea that every occupation (and not just the obviously spiritual ones) is holy if done "as unto the Lord" elevated the individual to a status seldom if ever experienced previously.

If Calvin and Luther were here today, they would be the first to

---

7. Richard DeVos, *Compassionate Capitalism: People Helping People Help Themselves* (New York: Penguin Books, 1993), p. 111.

8. Ibid., p. 172.

9. "Usury" refers to the charging of interest. Although the Bible has numerous passages that speak against charging a person interest on loans, Calvin allowed the practice when done by banks because, he felt, the sixteenth-century economy and the rise of institutions whose sole business was lending money created a different set of circumstances than that to which the relevant biblical texts were speaking. In the biblical world, it was wrong for a person to charge his or her friend interest. But for a bank, which can only survive by charging interest for its services, it was allowable. This teaching is just one of several from the Reformers that led to what Max Weber famously called "The Protestant Work Ethic," viewed by some as a key ingredient in America's early spirit and success.

decry the modern preoccupation with the Self — surely they never intended anything they wrote to contribute to such a "culture of narcissism." But what they did not foresee was that the spores of their own teachings would be wafted along by the winds of time, finally landing in the minds of others where they would germinate into some rather surprising individualistic plants.[10]

Calvin, Luther, and later Puritan teachers did indeed write much on the importance of the "lay life." But they hedged and qualified their teachings by pointing out that the individual was still under God and must, therefore, live for God's glory. When this was done, even ordinary service was holy. When, however, God's glory was not the goal, then even the holiest task was rendered useless and profane.

Still, the overarching idea was that it was possible for the individual to use his or her gifts in the world to glorify God. Charles Taylor puts it this way: "To take their proper place in God's order, humans had to avoid two opposite deviations: They must spurn the monkish error of renouncing the things of this world, for this amounts to scorning God's gifts. The other error was to become absorbed in things, take them for our end. . . . It was not the use of things that brought evil but our deviant purpose in using them."[11] So the Puritans came to speak of "weaned affections," that is, "having things as though having them not." We can enjoy and utilize the things of this life, but we do so with a measure of detachment by focusing on the God who gave them in the first place and then plying them toward his glory.

But once these teachings began to drift further into the larger culture, once they were untied from their specifically Christian, theological moorings, what remained was an unprecedented elevation of individual human work. Whereas in medieval times money, goods, commerce, and the like were to be shunned as "worldly," now they were touted as genuinely good things that a person could legitimately seek. Further, society came to be seen as a collection of individuals who could together shape that same society.

So if the very people who firmly taught all about grace likewise affirmed the goodness of ordinary life (and so helped foment a capitalist

10. Charles Taylor, *Sources of the Self* (Cambridge: Harvard University Press, 1989), pp. 211-33.

11. Ibid., p. 222.

spirit), why is this book, which celebrates Reformation teachings, also wary of the effects of capitalism? Once again I must emphasize that what I will attempt in this chapter is not a thoroughgoing critique of capitalism. Rather, its impetus is the thesis that the capitalism that the Reformation helped bring about is now undercutting the teaching on grace that brought about the Reformation!

In other words, in many places today we are witnessing a reversal of theological direction. In the sixteenth century the flow was mostly from the church to the culture. That is, theology and Scripture were used to evaluate, critique, or legitimate certain practices in the secular world. A proper, well-formed theology was the starting point from which was launched an evaluation of the business world, culture, and so on. It was the words of Scripture and the teaching on grace upon which Calvin and Luther based their subsequent teachings on the holiness of the everyday and the spiritual nature of every vocation.

Now, however, the main eddies and currents seem to be flowing the other direction. Authors such as David Wells and Os Guinness, among others, have noted that today the business world is primarily influencing the church and not the other way around. Increasingly, theology is not so much changing business practice as business practice is changing theology. Pastors are now referred to not as theologians-in-residence but as "spiritual CEOs." The traditional marks of the true church (pure preaching of the Word, proper exercise of the sacraments, and proper use of discipline) are being replaced by the marks of bottom-line results, increasing membership numbers, market share, and the like.

These days many pastors spend far less time pondering points of theology and far more time reading books on management technique. The stock-in-trade tools of many pastors's include not Greek and Hebrew but market surveys of their neighborhoods that reveal the kind of worship services people want (and hence the kind of service the modern pastor should tailor-make for that neighborhood). David Wells has noted that one of this country's most popular magazines for clergy devotes only about 1 percent of its articles to biblical/theological themes, with the other 99 percent being taken up by church management techniques, crisis management, and other such businesslike advice.[12]

---

12. David Wells, *No Place for Truth, or Whatever Happened to Evangelical Theology?* (Grand Rapids: Eerdmans, 1993), p. 114.

A recent *Christianity Today* poll asked people what they valued most in a pastor — which traits are important in making a pastor a "good" pastor. The poll revealed that although seminary professors still rate theological knowledge highest in importance, both pastors and laypersons rated theological knowledge the least important, with relational and management skills coming in at or near the top of their lists. *Christianity Today* also reported that today many seminaries "are intentionally using a business-world attitude to refocus attention on their 'customers.'"[13]

Thus worship services in many places are now nearly unrecognizable from what they were a generation ago. Fast-moving dramas have replaced sermons. Songbooks and hymnals have been shelved in favor of simpler choruses projected onto overhead screens. Collections have ceased altogether in some places so as not to offend those who view the church as being too money-grubbing. One Southern church was recently highlighted in the news for having a new "economy service" guaranteed to last no more than twenty minutes so that people could get in and out in a hurry — no fuss, no muss. As one writer recently noted, this is the "McChurch" approach — the ecclesiastical equivalent of a fast-food restaurant where you can have it "your way right away."

All these changes have come about because the business model is now seen as being the best model for churches to follow. Any smart capitalist knows that to succeed, you must "give the people what they want and how they want it" (and for the right price at that). So, success-oriented churches who now define that success by bottom-line profit margins and rising membership shares are going after the business model whole hog.

Now while, to a certain extent, the church of Jesus Christ has always contextualized itself and its message in order to be understood, and while the church can doubtless learn many good things from the business world, today in some places churches appear to have gone beyond adopting this or adapting to that. As Os Guinness notes, "[T]he slippage in truth and theology, in creeds and doctrines, indicates that more than just this or that aspect of modernity is being picked up and used. We're accommodating ourselves to the whole package."[14]

13. *Christianity Today* 38.12 (October 24, 1994): 74-78.

14. Os Guinness, *Dining with the Devil* (Grand Rapids: Baker Books, 1993), p. 24.

As I said before, the purpose of this book is not to critique these trends per se. (Anyway, David Wells's *No Place for Truth* [Grand Rapids: Eerdmans, 1993] and *God in the Wasteland* [Grand Rapids: Eerdmans, 1994] along with Os Guinness's *Dining with the Devil* [Grand Rapids: Baker, 1993], have already presented outstanding and thoughtful critiques of modernizing worship and theology. Readers interested in these topics should read these books.) But I mention these trends to substantiate the thesis that whereas the Reformation used theology to guide and critique commerce and capitalism, we are now using commerce and capitalism to guide and critique theology and church practice. Thus I ask again: What effect has the spirit of democratic capitalism had on our churches, our Sunday school programs, our families? If these other trends are any indication, the answer to that question could be, "Quite a large effect, indeed!"

To deal with this complex matter, we will proceed as follows: First, we will look at a brief sketch of the nature of democratic capitalism. What is it? What are its ideals, its "world-and-life view," its dreams? Second, we will examine examples of how democratic capitalism has influenced our culture generally, but more especially what impact it has had on our churches and families as part of that culture. What kinds of practices do we engage in without even realizing that they stem more from a spirit of capitalism than from a spirit of grace? Finally, we will consider a number of practical suggestions to reverse the stream, so that theology may once again be what guides us; along with that, we will try to come up with some suggestions as to how businesspeople, pastors, Sunday school teachers, and Christian parents can resist teaching works righteousness and key instead on the grace of God alone.

Capitalism: What Is It?

Simply put, capitalism is an economic theory and system for the gathering, management, and distribution of capital. In this economic system, people try to create wealth through fostering business and commerce in free and open markets. The capital that is in view here is not simply money (though perhaps principally that), but it also includes such things as the means of production, labor, and labor-producing and labor-fomenting structures. More to the point, democratic capitalism

94

is, according to Michael Novak, "three systems in one: a predominantly market economy; a polity respectful of the rights of the individual to life, liberty, and the pursuit of happiness; and a system of cultural institutions moved by ideals of liberty and justice for all."[15]

Central to most definitions of democratic capitalism is the idea of individual freedom or liberty. "The word capital comes from the Latin and means 'wealth.' Capitalism is an economic system based on the free accumulation of capital or wealth. The main characteristics of capitalism are private ownership of capital and freedom of enterprise."[16] In democratic capitalism, people are left alone to develop, to the best of their abilities, their various gifts, talents, ideas, projects, and ventures. In fact, a key component in capitalism, as envisioned by a pioneer in the field, Adam Smith, was the idea of laissez-faire, which means that the government "lets people do" what they wish with minimal (preferably no) outside interference. Thus the individual truly must take the initiative and provide his or her own drive, incentive, and capital to get a project off the ground.

My hometown is Ada, Michigan — a sleepy little village that remarkably is home to one of the world's largest and most successful privately owned corporations: Amway. Set in the center of Amway's sprawling mile-and-a-half industrial complex is "The Center of Free Enterprise" — a monument to the entrepreneurial spirit of America on which Amway (the *"American Way"*) was founded. Indeed, the fundamental thesis of Amway cofounder Rich DeVos is that the individual can do it and must do it. Only the freedom of our democratic system allows people to dream dreams and then realize them through hard work, effort, initiative, and personal drive.

What we need, according to DeVos, is "freedom to become complete and whole persons. The freedom to become what God intends all of us to be. The freedom of mind and imagination that can only exist in a truly democratic society. The freedom not just to scrape by, but to find genuine satisfaction in life."[17] Although DeVos promotes a "compassionate capitalism" that respects persons through remembering the image of God in them (and he makes some good points, which

15. Novak, *The Spirit of Democratic Capitalism*, p. 14.
16. DeVos, *Compassionate Capitalism*, p. 104.
17. Ibid., p. 5.

will be noted below), the subtitle of his book still points to the fundamental American belief that people are finally responsible for making
it on their own: *Compassionate Capitalism: People Helping People Help
Themselves* (emphasis mine). In DeVos's own words, "In a truly compassionate system, all effort is directed toward making people indepen-
dent and capable of standing on their own two feet."[18]

Capitalism, then, is that complex system by which individuals are
allowed to contribute to the larger society through the free exercise of
their gifts. Clearly the individual is the key, an emphasis that has
troubled several Christian writers. In the past, some of them have touted
a form of socialism as being a more Christian system than the privatistic
setup that seems inherent in capitalism.

A number of writers have alleged that socialism, with its emphasis
on sharing and community, seems better to reflect New Testament
church patterns as well as general scriptural advice on matters like
treating the poor fairly. But others today (notably Michael Novak and
Richard John Neuhaus) hotly refute such ideas, holding that the freedom and dignity accorded to individuals in democratically capitalist
systems is more reflective of human dignity than the manipulative,
controlling ways of some socialist systems.

Whatever one might make of such theoretical debates, the mere
fact that such disputes exist highlights nicely the fact that a focus on
free individuals and their need to make it on their own (or fail on their
own) lies close to the heart of the capitalist spirit. That this is so can
be seen in certain statements of even some Christian thinkers.

We have already noted that Rich DeVos, although he has many
fine ideas for granting people dignity as God's image-bearers, still
repeatedly considers the individual as finally responsible for his or her
success or failure. He views even a "compassionate" treatment of workers and customers as the best way to increase productivity and so be a
financial success. As he notes in *Compassionate Capitalism*, "We are
created to dream. Our dreams, too, are created in the image of God's
dreams. . . . We are loved by God and empowered by our Creator to
see our dreams come true."[19] Again, "Remember, it's only the beginning
to say, 'I want to do something better.' Dreaming is the first step of a

18. Ibid., p. 268.
19. Ibid., pp. 22-23.

lifelong trek away from mediocrity and failure, toward accomplishment and a sense of fulfillment and self-worth. And it's compassionate capitalism that helps make that journey possible."[20]

Capitalism: Its Larger Effects

As economic policy goes, these kinds of sentiments are probably correct. But now we must move from economics toward theology to see where the former may be infecting (and altering) the latter. Already in DeVos's comments we can detect a subtle but curious shift: the goal of human life, of divine image-bearing, is not "glorifying God and enjoying him forever" (the Westminster Confession's well-known answer to the goal of human life), but fulfilling our own dreams and so feeling fulfilled as a result of that fine effort.

In a striking passage in his book *The Spirit of Democratic Capitalism*, Michael Novak likewise crosses the line from economics to theology with, to say the least, unsettling results. Having written about the fundamental good of democratic capitalism for over 300 pages, Novak wraps up his work by pointing to six theological areas that he feels support or at least illumine democratic capitalism — strikingly, however, the gospel core of grace is not one of those areas. But then comes a key distortion: "A political economy needs bold political leaders who thrive on contests of power and willful dreamers and builders who delight in overcoming economic difficulties in order to produce. The will-to-power must be made creative, not destroyed. In this respect, Judaism and Christianity are religions of narrative and liberty. Judaism and Christianity, in other words, *envisage human life as a contest.* The stakes are real; there are winners and losers."[21]

Granted that Novak is not saying that we save ourselves. He does write a bit further on that "even those who are 'elected' are so through God's grace, not through any initiative or power of their own; still, each is free to say yes or no."[22] Granted that Novak admits that "success

20. Ibid., p. 47.
21. Novak, *The Spirit of Democratic Capitalism*, pp. 344-45 (emphasis mine).
22. Ibid., p. 345.

in this world is often entirely the opposite of success in the life of grace."[23] Granted, in short, that Novak is not holding out for some kind of works righteousness strictly understood. Still, are "competition" and "contests" words that well sum up the gospel? Is it "wrong to imagine that the spirit of competition is foreign to the gospels," as Novak asserts?[24] It is worth pondering.

For contests, as I understand them, are affairs with winners and losers in which the goal is to do all you can to become the one and avoid becoming the other. Contests rely on the strength, training, willpower, brainpower, cleverness, and maneuvering of the participants, with the winners being those with more strength, more training, more willpower, and the like.

Christianity, as I understand it, says that life is first of all a gift — a gift we humans in fact mishandle and spoil, but it is a life that we receive back again as a gift of grace through Jesus Christ, who did what we could never do (paid the price for sin) so that we might be saved from the worst part of our own sinful selves. Jesus did it because we could not — not ever. Jesus died because we were dead in our sins — and being dead does not place one in a position to compete (or even to say "Yes" to God if he had not first made us "alive in Christ" and so enabled us to say "Yes").

If grace is what the gospel is finally all about, it is a little hard to understand how the image of a contest could help us get a grip on the gospel message. A contest may be a fine image for success in the business world, but when imported into the theological realm, it is the equivalent of a massive heart attack — the gospel keels over dead in its tracks as

---

23. Ibid., p. 345.

24. Of course, there is a New Testament motif of Christ's doing battle with "the powers and principalities" of this world. Furthermore, there is the theme of the Christian's doing battle with the forces of darkness and hence the need to be outfitted with the armor of faith. But while this could be viewed as a kind of "contest," such spiritual battles are surely of a rather different nature than, say, a football game or corporate striving in the business world. Also, the Bible teaches that the Christian can fight and win not because of any power of his or her own but only because Christ has already won the battle and empowers believers in their own struggles with temptation. Such a teaching is radically discontinuous with any idea that Christians compete to win a prize or reward that would not otherwise be theirs.

soon as we start to envisage it as a contest in which we must dream something and then do it via our own will-to-power. Novak may be correct in stating that within the bounds of human life, competitions and contests are things on which we thrive, but that hardly means that competition is what the Christian story is finally (or even mostly) all about!

The point is that the capitalist spirit — with its focus on the individual, its touting of freedom, its insistence that we all make it on our own — is so pervasive a phenomenon in America that theology is likely to be infected with it. When that occurs, it is to the detriment of a pure apprehension of God's grace in Christ. God's grace, and our utter need for it, tells us that without outside help, without Someone's doing it all for us, we are lost. Capitalism says that outside interference is a bad thing and that only personal achievement counts for anything.

Indeed, to a capitalist, one of the most detested notions is that anyone should get a "free ride" in life. The good things in life should be earned through hard work and should not merely be given to the undeserving. (I recently heard someone suggest that we should even put a cap on how much a person should be able to inherit.) This idea comes up most commonly when the welfare state is being discussed. Again, we will not be debating the ins and outs of welfare — but it may be instructive to note the up-front disdain that most Americans have for anything not earned.[25]

Granted that welfare as it has been exercised in this country has its problems (fostering of undue dependency, abuse of the system, and so on). But it seems that what some Christians find most repugnant about welfare is not the abuse of the system per se, but the mere idea of a giveaway.

Separating theology from economics is perhaps nowhere more snarled than here. But take note: The heart of the New Testament beats with the message that we have all received a free gift from God — salvation. We did nothing to earn it, we did not deserve it, God simply

25. We are focusing here on "the culture of capitalism." Of course, within our society we now also have what some call "the culture of entitlement" and "the culture of victims." These subcultures in America may fight against biblical grace in quite different ways than does the capitalist ethos. Still, I believe that capitalism, classically understood, is the overarching ethos of this society, and that is why I have targeted it as the subject for this chapter.

gave it to us because he loved us and because he knew that without it we would never make it back home.

Grace *is* a giveaway, a free ride to eternal life. Grace helps those who flat out could not help themselves. The implication of this theological truth need not be that economically we also give everything away. However, if we are Christians who are saved by grace, we need to ponder long and hard what it is about welfare that so perturbs us (if we are in fact perturbed by it). If we are genuinely concerned for would-be welfare recipients and want to help them in a more complete way than merely giving them money, we are thinking economically *and* compassionately. We might then be in a position to help them in more constructive ways.

However, if we think that all forms of welfare are a bad idea — that no one should ever be forgiven a debt, gotten out of a jam, bridged to a better life without thought of repayment — what does that attitude say about our overall attitudes toward life and, yes, toward the gospel? Walter Block criticizes the welfare state because "it creates dependence; and it reduces self-reliance."[26] Economically this may be so. However, theologically, Christians should never think that dependence (on God) and a lack of self-reliance are by themselves bad things. Unless we acknowledge our wholesale dependence on God and renounce any attempt to rely on ourselves where salvation is concerned, we will not understand grace and so will find ourselves in the fix of the Rich Young Man.

Where Christians are able fully and appropriately to separate how they are saved in Christ from how they succeed economically, none of this has much relevance.[27] But if, as I believe is the case, we tend to allow the economic to influence the theological, all of this needs some careful sorting out by any thoughtful Christian who wishes truly to sing out and live out the glories of God's gracious salvation.

Doing this, however, may not be as easy as we at times think. For the simple fact is that in our day-to-day lives, in what we listen to on

26. Quoted in Berger, ed., *The Capitalist Spirit*, p. 114.

27. Note that I am *not* suggesting that theology and economics should never intertwine, that they are separate realms with no intersection. Christians in business, for instance, must think theologically about their work and not cordon off the labor of Monday through Saturday from worship on Sunday. I am not saying that we should not think theologically about economics but only that we should be exceedingly wary of thinking economically about theology.

the radio, in what we view on television or at the movies, in what we read and in how we converse, precious little (if anything) reminds us of grace. We find very little that is a genuine giveaway. Our heroes are usually athletic "winners" and business "successes" but rarely gracious givers. Simply put, very little reminds us of grace on a daily basis.

There are, however, a large number of ideas and images to remind us of a capitalistic earning of rewards or meriting of failures. The result, according to William Dyrness, is "The central irony that in spite of the massive influence of Christianity on American middle-class culture, no primary metaphor exists that captures the central dynamic of Christianity. Indeed, there is almost no instance in our culture in which we are aware of absolute limits which require some kind of sacrificial intervention. We may plunge in and lend a hand, we may try our best to scratch out the dirtiness, but in the end everyone must 'do their own time.' "[28] The great American ideal, with the heroes of the past and present who embody it, is to make it on one's own with little or no outside help. Every person is responsible for his or her own self, and no one else can do the work of another.

Foreign missionaries frequently relate that upon arriving in a native culture, they sometimes find a central image, prominent myth, or current practice that all indigenous people know and that in turn helps them to relate to Jesus' sacrifice and God's gracious salvation. In other words, something about their cultural ethos and experience makes it easier for them to understand the gospel's talk of grace — of one person's sacrifice for the sake of others.

For instance, missionaries to New Guinea once reported on the "peace child" — a tradition whereby the chiefs of warring tribes would settle their disputes by exchanging children. Each chief would then raise the other chief's child and so be constantly reminded of the need to keep the peace for the sake of his own child who was still in the camp of his tribe's one-time enemy. When the story of Jesus' being graciously sent to our world as an infant was told to these people, they had a way to relate.[29] Jesus was God's "peace child" to bring and then keep the peace between

---

28. William Dyrness, *How Does America Hear the Gospel?* (Grand Rapids: Eerdmans, 1989), p. 13.

29. Quoted from "Landmarks" curriculum material (Grand Rapids: Christian Reformed Publications, 1991).

God and humanity. Likewise Dyrness tells of an Alaskan tribe whose chief once saved the lives of ten of his tribesmen by offering his life for theirs — a chief's life, after all, was worth the lives of at least ten ordinary folks. When this tribe heard of Jesus' sacrifice to save humanity, they had a quick way to relate to it because it was so similar to this national story of sacrifice. The one died for the many.[30]

But, Dyrness asserts, not so in America. Our heroes are not generally noble martyrs or gracious gift-givers. America's mythic heroes are rugged individualists — rags-to-riches types who use their abilities to get themselves ahead in the world. American heroes are those with a limitless sense of their own abilities; the kinds of people (à la Ronald Reagan in the early 1980s) who say things like, "There's nothing we cannot do!" Indeed, in his memoirs, President Jimmy Carter noted that once he began to speak to the American people about limits (limits to natural resources, energy, spending, and the like), he began to lose political ground. Already in his inaugural speech Carter stated that "We have learned that 'more' is not necessarily 'better,' that even our great nation has its recognized limits, and that we can neither answer all questions nor solve all problems . . . we must simply do our best." Alas, however, Carter noted the simple fact that "Americans were not accustomed to limits."[31]

Much more in keeping with American belief in the limitless possibilities of the individual was the message four years later of Ronald Reagan. Biographer Lou Cannon observes that what came across in Reagan's speeches well typified the man. For Reagan "preached love of country, distrust of government, the glories of economic opportunity, the dangers of regulating business and the wonders of free markets and free trade. He believed in the manifest destiny of the United States of America."[32] It was the spirit of this message, and not Carter's more measured tone, that captured the imagination of the electorate in 1980. For Reagan asked Americans to " 'dream heroic dreams' and to discard what he considered the corrosive pessimism of the Carter years."[33]

30. Dyrness, *How Does America Hear the Gospel?* p. 10.
31. Jimmy Carter, *Keeping Faith* (New York: Bantam Books, 1982), p. 21.
32. Lou Cannon, *President Reagan: Role of a Lifetime* (New York: Simon and Schuster, 1991), p. 34.
33. Ibid., p. 22.

There are, of course, many complex reasons why the vast majority of Christians supported Reagan's message in 1980. However, Garry Wills once remarked that, despite the fact that Carter's message was more in keeping with a biblical theology of original sin and the need for grace, it was Reagan's message of limitlessness and a can-do spirit that seemed better to accord with the understanding of even many Christians. When the religious Right became disillusioned with Carter's social stands and international policies, Reagan came and wooed them with the assurance, "We're number one."[34]

But perhaps this, too, is not surprising. Evangelical historians like Mark Noll and Nathan Hatch have repeatedly demonstrated that there has long been a snug link between American Christianity and American democratic ideals. Nathan Hatch in particular has adroitly traced out the deep, abiding populism of American Christianity. For instance, a hallmark of nineteenth-century religious practice in America was a shunning of established theological authority (including professionally trained clergy) and an embracing of self-made, self-taught preachers like Charles Finney.[35]

Even in church life American Christians gave in to the egalitarian, populist spirit of the nation by preferring those who had made it all on their own. Hatch suggests that the democratization of Christianity was driven by three factors: A distrust of established theological authority in favor of self-made individuals, an empowering of ordinary people to validate their own religious life through experience, and an exceedingly optimistic sense of the limitless possibilities of what could be achieved through the efforts of ordinary folk.[36]

Likewise, in a trenchant analysis of the American evangelical scene, Mark Noll recently asserted that the early history of Christianity in America was characterized by an uncritical adaptation of Christian conviction to American ideals (what he calls a "Christian-Cultural Synthesis"). He further contends that this alignment of American democracy with Christianity persists today. The main result Noll perceives is an atrophy of the evangelical mind — after all, the more one assumes Christianity and

---

34. Garry Wills, *Under God* (New York: Simon and Schuster, 1990), pp. 119-20.

35. Nathan Hatch, *The Democratization of American Christianity* (New Haven: Yale University Press, 1989), pp. 196ff.

36. Ibid., pp. 9-10.

American ideals to be compatible, the less likely one is to think critically about such matters as our culture and our politics. As Noll himself puts it, "[T]he assumption that Christian faith can be expressed fully and properly only in a democratic setting was not conducive to shaping a Christian mind. Because evangelicals so thoroughly assumed the harmony of Christian faith and democratic America, they did not think comprehensively and foundationally about very real problems."[37] This same uncritical transference of ideas from culture to theology may also short-circuit a pure, biblical apprehension of grace.

For America, in ways both definable and not, is driven by the spirit of democratic capitalism. Capitalism's focus on freedom, its insistence on the individual's potential, responsibility, and possibilities, and its limitless can-do attitude toward all of life have affected (or, perhaps better said, infected) American Christians and their attitudes toward grace and theology. That most voting Christians in 1980 would be turned off by a message of limits and energized by one of limitlessness is but one small symptom of this larger malaise.[38]

William Dyrness is right: Americans have no central metaphor by

37. Mark Noll, *The Scandal of the Evangelical Mind* (Grand Rapids: Eerdmans, 1994), p. 74.

38. When I have presented these ideas to others, some have gotten the impression that I am being "anti-America." But it should be clear that my intention is not to write a critique of capitalism, so also I do not intend to rail against American culture or suggest that it is deeply flawed. The simple fact is that America is a land of opportunity and freedom — a place where individuals have the lovely chance to make a living and live a life for themselves and their families, where ordinary citizens can rise to the Oval Office, where personal drive and ambition can be rewarded through economic success, and so on. All of these are fine aspects of our country, and I am not suggesting otherwise. The point here should be clear: The problem is not capitalism or the American cultural ethos but rather the influence they can come to have on theology and the church. It is one thing for the broader culture to celebrate freedom, independence, and personal achievement; it is quite another matter if those same ideas come to inform or deform our ideas of how we are saved. Most people recognize that our culture's negative facets — for instance, the current "anything goes" ethic of sexuality — can produce a challenge for the church and its attempts to be distinctive. But sometimes even a culture's positive aspects can provide a challenge, as I believe is the case with keeping clear our understanding of grace in a place where almost everything else is earned.

which to express or hook up to the gospel; the American ethos, fueled and driven by capitalist ideals, centers on the power of the individual to "do it!" Americans would be hard pressed to find a hero who, on the order of the Alaskan chief, exemplified the grace of the gospel.[39]

But does any of this spirit of can-do democratic capitalism really enter the Christian church or home in any specific ways? Are there identifiable examples that in these vital places there is more a sense of works righteousness than one of grace? Indeed, there are. Let us now turn our attention to these vital arenas, keying most especially on the ways in which the church and the family nurture children. For if children do not get the message of grace from an early age, they will be unlikely to grow into gracious adults.

Unhappily, the effects of our culture's love affair with capitalist ways are on display in churches — sometimes in obvious ways, sometimes in very subtle ones. On the more obvious side are the high-profile congregations, especially those featured on television. Because television is an audience-driven medium, and because people would rather hear stories of success than confessions of sinful weakness and failure, television ministries such as Robert Schuller's generally feature a parade of "winners."[40] Schuller's church services generally feature a guest celebrity of the week. Mostly these are from among "the beautiful people" of

---

39. A friend of mine once suggested that Abraham Lincoln might be such a hero — he gave freedom to slaves and was martyred for his effort. There may be something to this, but in my experience, when people speak of Lincoln they rarely mention the fact that he freed the slaves in a gracious, selfless manner, but rather that he was the "self-made man," the rail-splitter who started in a log cabin, educated himself by candlelight, and made a great success out of his life. This rags-to-riches scenario, a largely embellished myth according to Lincoln biographer Stephen Oates, is what people key on first, and any good actions he may have executed as President were little more than by-products of his self-made success. The mere fact that Lincoln's rags-to-riches story is greatly embellished is itself telling in terms of what Americans like to see in a person and hence emulate in themselves.

40. Robert Schuller's theology of self-esteem, with its endemic "possibility thinking," is itself a reflection of the capitalist "You can do it!" ethos reflected in the writing of Rich DeVos and other promoters of capitalism. It is thus not surprising that when Robert Schuller spoke at my high school chapel some years ago, he was introduced by Rich DeVos!

nearby Hollywood — glamorous folks with a story of success to tell by which they inspire others to likewise "be all that they can be."

Other such examples from the glitzy world of televangelism could easily be multiplied. But the sum of it is well put by Quentin Schultze: "Americans are optimistic, and so is their television. On television it is not God that saves, but good sense, luck, patience, power, or money. [So also] the faith of some televangelists is more American than Christian, more popular than historic, more personal than collective, and more experiential than biblical." In short, Schultze asserts, "They reflect the American Dream."[41]

But perhaps by now, given the well-documented scandals of TV preachers, most people would react to this by saying, "Well, what would you expect from *them?* Such things could never happen in our local churches." So what about closer to home — what about within our own congregations and Sunday school classrooms, or around our own dinner tables? Surely in these places grace has no difficulty getting through to our children. Or does it? We want to communicate to our children that God loves them just because. We want them to grow up knowing that because of Jesus, God loves them no matter how bad they are or how badly they behave. We want them to know that the basis for that assurance is not their behavior but God's love alone. We want them to know about unconditional grace — the grace in which they were baptized even when they were too little to know or do anything!

But what happens to those ideas when we also ask them to sing songs like, "Oh, be careful little hands what you do. . . . For the Father up above is looking down in love, so be careful little hands what you do"? What happens to our words about God's unconditional love when children perceive that the only way to earn the Sunday school teacher's approval (whether that is evidenced through loving words, a gold star on a chart, or a candy bar) is to toe the line and memorize the verse? What happens to a child's concept of God's unconditional, gracious love when a mother constantly tells her daughter, "What would Jesus say if he saw you doing that?"

What kind of message is communicated to children when, all the

---

41. Quentin Schultze, *Televangelism and American Culture* (Grand Rapids: Baker Book House, 1991), pp. 116, 132-33.

while they are growing up, they see a plaque on the wall that solemnly warns them to watch their step lest they be somewhere bad "when Jesus comes again"? What happens to young people's sense of grace if, throughout the course of their adolescence, they hear their ministers preaching against the sins of the flesh but not giving at least equal time to God's gracious forgiveness for failure? What happens to grace when children observe seemingly peerless ministers and adults who refuse honestly to admit their own struggles with sin or to acknowledge the complexities of a fallen world in which we need God's grace not just to forgive us but to help us survive?[42]

What happens is that at least some children *hear* about grace, but they *experience* only a kind of instruction driven by an earning of rewards or a meriting of punishments. What happens is that the grace we teach is eclipsed by the works righteousness we live. When all of that is combined with the thoroughgoing capitalist spirit in society outside the church, an awareness of grace may be lost for children altogether.

My seminary professor of education, Dr. Marion Snapper, was well known for his thoughts on what he called "C-Content" and "P-Content." Anyone involved in teaching or raising children would do well to pay attention to the distinction. C-Content, according to Snapper, is the "Content content" of education: matters such as the historical dates you memorize, the verses you learn, and the multiplication tables you work through. C-Content is what the teacher explicitly teaches. It is what is found in the textbook, on the worksheet, on the blackboard, or on the computer screen.

P-Content is "Process Content" — this is what a teacher (or parent) teaches implicitly via his or her own actions or attitudes, which come through to the student on an indirect level. So in a history class, for example, "C-Content" would be the teacher's saying, "Today we are going to learn about the Civil War — we will memorize key dates, battle sites, the role of President Lincoln, and more." P-Content would be what the class senses from the teacher about history generally and the Civil War specifically. Is the teacher enthusiastic about his or her subject?

42. Some of the ideas in this section originally came from Donald Sloat's fine book *The Dangers of Growing Up in a Christian Home* (Nashville: Thomas Nelson Publishers, 1986).

Does the teacher think deep in his or her own soul that this information is so vital that he or she cannot wait to pass it along to the students? Or does even the teacher, like many of the students, think that this is crashingly dull? Is the teacher feeling flat, bored, worn-out by life and by the tediousness of his or her own subject matter, or is he or she alive, sparkling, and energetic about the wonderful task of teaching and shaping young minds? The one attitude can infect the students with a measure of enthusiasm and a positive attitude toward history; the other attitude, if caught and picked up on by the students, will induce intellectual torpor.

In other words, P-Content is the stuff of personal experience in a teacher or parent. This is the content of the process, that which is not taught but caught. What ought to be properly humbling and frightening to anyone who teaches is Snapper's contention that it is the P-Content, not C-Content, that sticks with the student the longest. C-Content learning is generally passive — you merely pour, or allow another to pour, information into your head — you memorize the dates, learn the tables, and the rest. But because P-Content depends on keen observation and personal experience, it is a more active kind of learning. Because it is more all-involving for the student, P-Content learning sticks with the student longer. The feelings linger longer than the data.

In relation to the teaching of grace, this means that a Sunday school teacher can talk about the free grace of God with his or her students, and even have the students memorize a verse like, "For it is by grace that you have been saved . . . ," but while the content of the verse or teaching might eventually fade for a student, the fact of memorizing it in order to earn a piece of candy will not. The child may *hear* words about grace, but will *experience* working for rewards and getting only what one deserves or earns.

So, too, in the Christian home. As Donald Sloat observes in his *The Dangers of Growing Up in a Christian Home*, "[T]he way parents treat their children in daily living has more impact on their children's eventual spiritual development than the family's religious practices, including having family altar, reading the Bible together, attending church services together, and so on."[43] Christian homes that produce

43. Ibid., p. 81.

guilt are not likely to overcome that by saying words about grace. Christian churches in which ministers speak much of sin but little of grace, much of the mistakes of others but little of their own earnest struggles, likewise produce more guilt for sin than gratitude for grace.

A genuinely tragic feature of all this, of course, is that few parents or Sunday school teachers intend to do any harm to grace. The mother who tells her son, "What would Jesus say if . . . " is trying to be very devout and religious with her son and doubtless understands those words as a proper fulfillment of the vows she took at the child's baptism.[44] The Sunday school teacher who offers rewards based on performance is not trying to undercut grace but only to find ways to motivate the children to memorize the most important book they will ever run across — the Bible! If a preacher forgets to mention grace in his enthusiasm for delineating sin, he may be derelict, but he is doing so out of a deep concern to help young people (and adults) be better people for God. Sometimes we preachers even do this, simply assuming that everyone realizes that an emphasis on proper behavior is in the context of our saying "Thank You" to God for grace. That is, we assume that everyone knows that how we act does not get us to heaven but is a result of having already been brought there by the grace of Christ (see Chapter Two). But I wonder how many people always recall that distinction and do not need to be reminded directly and with routine regularity?

Undercutting grace and giving in to the pervasive capitalist, pull-yourself-up-by-your-own-bootstraps mentality is as unintentional as it is devastating. Having grown up in a culture whose heroes are rugged, rags-to-riches individualists, having grown up listening to presidents who hawked the American dream and preachers who also thought it was the way to go, having seen in a multitude of ways that self-reliance is good and undue dependence is bad — having seen all that, we have learned our lessons well. We Christians, too, have learned more P-Content than C-Content when it comes to God's grace and the way one receives life's greatest rewards.

44. Ibid., p. 77.

Recapturing Grace

In a multitude of ways, therefore, the American spirit makes it hard for us to know about and accept God's grace as our only way to salvation. The idea that we must each "make it on our own," the seeking after rewards (and the proffering of rewards to motivate right behavior), and the overarching goal of personal success as the purpose of human life are difficult ideas to transcend in our culture. Assuming, however, that we Christians do not wish to violate and vitiate the gospel's core message of grace, what can we do to keep grace in focus? Recognizing that we cannot change the entire capitalist system (indeed, recognizing that there may be many good things about capitalism from a purely economic point of view), what can we do in the midst of capitalism to sharpen and focus the message of grace for ourselves and for our children?

What follows is a list of specific suggestions for businesspersons, teachers, parents, and pastors. As I stated in the Introduction, I make no claims of presenting exhaustive lists of suggestions. The following are rudimentary ideas, some starters to get us thinking about still more ways we can teach and live grace. So first I will attempt to make some general suggestions for anyone to keep in mind as he or she lives day by day in a capitalist society. Some of these will be drawn directly from the Bible and its views of capital and wealth, but others will be drawn from more diverse sources based on broader biblical principles. First, a few general suggestions.

Whether you are involved in business or not, you are a part of an economy that, as a rule, pays out what it owes — no more, no less. If you collect a paycheck every week, you, too, are involved on a regular basis in doing your work for the primary purpose of earning that check and so providing for yourself and/or your family. Is there a way, even in the midst of all this earning and rewarding, to remind ourselves of God's grace? Perhaps the biblical book of Deuteronomy can be of help in this regard.

Deuteronomy is in many ways one very long sermon from Moses. The generation who had been led out of Egypt and who had stood at Mount Sinai during the giving of the Law was now dead. The next generation of children and grandchildren were now on the plains of Moab, the very lip of the Promised Land. But before they entered that "good land flowing with milk and honey," Moses wanted to remind them of God's ways.

There was an urgency to Moses' grand sermon. For Moses knew that during the rigors of the wilderness period, remembering God's presence and blessings had been comparatively easy. After all, the wilderness is a hard, chaotic place. Water and food are scarce, while scorpions and sandstorms are plentiful. So while in the wilderness, the people had to depend on God or be consumed. Surely the daily manna on the desert floor, as well as the miracles of water from a rock, birds dropping from the sky, and God's presence in the cloudy or fiery pillar all served as reminders to the people that they were dependent on God alone (though even in the desert the people regularly grumbled, complained, and missed the significance of certain divine interventions of providence).

But soon they would be in the Promised Land. Soon they would raise their own food and bake their own bread and thus not need manna. Soon they would draw water from smartly dug wells and not need to see rocks split miraculously. Soon they would no longer see the cloudy and fiery pillars. Soon they would be tempted to say, "My power and the strength of my hands have produced this wealth for me" (Deut. 8:17).

So throughout Deuteronomy, in addition to reminding the people of God's Law and guidelines for living, Moses shouts out again and again, "Remember and do not forget!" The people were to recall God's special graces during the wilderness period in order to realize that God's presence and God's grace were still present in the Promised Land. They were to remember that water from a well was no less a sign of God's grace (his lovingkindness) than was water from a rock; that vines heavy with grapes were no less a sign of God's goodness than was manna appearing out of nowhere; that strong backs, healthy families, and fat bank accounts were just as vivid a reminder of God's abiding presence as had been those cloudy, fiery pillars. In short, they were to remember God's big, stunning graces of the past in order to be able to recognize his abiding, ordinary graces in the present. If they forgot that, Moses warned, they would inevitably begin to worship other gods — starting with their own selves.

For all of us who live and work in a good land flowing with fast food and consumer goods, this is a timely reminder. How easy to collect

111

our paychecks and pat only ourselves on the back for them. How easy to peruse the glutted aisles of a supermarket or survey the crowded shelves of our own pantries without ever realizing that all these good things are the little graces of God that ultimately spin out of the big Grace that is Jesus Christ.

We, along with the Israelites of old, need to remember and not forget. We need to remember that all good things — our gifts, our abilities, our capital — come from above. We need to sense God's presence in the everyday; we need (as Frederick Buechner always encourages us) to "listen to our lives for the sound of him." We need to live alive to the grace with which the cosmos sings and by which our every blessing comes. Doing so may help qualify our sense of having "made it" purely on our own. Perhaps we have been good stewards of our gifts and so have gained a certain amount of wealth. As I said in Chapter Two, we should be thankful for that, but we must also never forget its source. The good things in our lives ought to inspire all the more gratitude to the gracious God who gave them all.

One other note in general before moving on to more specific suggestions: Certain Old Testament practices can remind us of the One to whom all our capital finally belongs and of the fact that we are therefore to manage it on his behalf. Among the laws and commands of which Moses spoke in Deuteronomy were matters such as the Jubilee and the sabbatical years. Israel was to allow fields to "rest" every seven years — to allow them to lie fallow for one year as a reminder that "the earth is the LORD's, and everything in it" (Ps. 24:1) and that they were little more than tenants on God's land.

Every fiftieth year they were to celebrate the Jubilee — a time in which all debts were to be cancelled and all foreclosed property was to be returned to the family of the original owners. This, too, was a reminder that God was concerned for all people and that, while he encouraged use of gifts and accumulation of goods, that was not the final goal of human life before God. Fairness, justice, and equity for all were more important than excessive riches for a few. (Unhappily, Israel did not follow these laws. Thus prophets like Amos lambasted the people and saw nothing but unjust chaos in the land — a chaos for which punishment followed.)

We, too, would do well to recall that our capital, our goods, and our land are but loans from the God to whom they belong ultimately and proximately. How we manage these things on the Master's behalf, how we view our wealth, and how we share it with those who have less have profound implications for us spiritually. (It may also have profound economic implications, but that is the subject for a different book.) So we must remember the "grace of the everyday." If we do so, our own efforts, in the business world as well as everywhere else, will themselves be qualified by God's overarching grace in Christ. "It is God who works in you to will and to act according to his good purpose" (Phil. 2:13).

But now for some concrete suggestions, first of all for Christians who are in the "business of business." If you are an employer, what kinds of attitudes can you foster within yourself and what kind of atmosphere can you create for your employees that will, even in the midst of profit-making and paying attention to the "bottom line," nonetheless remind you and them of grace? Perhaps one key item to keep in mind is that your employees are people created in God's image and that they have worth that extends beyond whatever they are able to produce for you (or, conversely, whatever they may be *unable* to produce). In the world of economics, those who produce more will get paid more — more money, more attention, and so on. But in the world of theology, a Christian must find a different way of reckoning ultimate value.

As Rich DeVos points out, "What we think about people matters a great deal. If we think of them as children of God, possessing a divine spark and having God-given worth, it follows that we ought to treat all people with respect and dignity."[45]

While a businessperson must manage with an eye toward profits (after all, bad management resulting in a failed company will benefit neither the boss nor the soon-to-be-unemployed workers), ways can be found to be sensitive to people as people — to take an interest in them and to show concern for them beyond what they can do for you. As Pope John Paul II adeptly points out, "[T]here are many human needs that find no place on the market. [P]rofitability is not the only indicator of a firm's condition. It is possible for the financial accounts to be in order, and yet for the people — who are the firm's most valuable asset — to be humiliated and their dignity offended. This is morally inad-

---

45. DeVos, *Compassionate Capitalism*, p. 5.

missible. The purpose of a business firm is to be a community of persons endeavoring to satisfy basic needs at the service of the whole society."[46]

The specific way in which such care is expressed and such a "community" is built is largely up to the individual employer. But the point is that in light of God's grace in Christ employees deserve to be accorded worth, love, and respect simply for who they are — which is a Godlike way of viewing persons and a Christlike way of treating them. Employees are always finally more than mere means of production.

In the play and film *Glengarry Glen Ross* we witness the grim spectacle of what happens when employers lose sight of this. The story takes place in a real estate firm where the salesmen must either produce a certain quota of sales or be fired. At one point a higher-up from the downtown office comes in to deliver a marrow-chilling speech in which he degrades the individual salesmen because of their low sales and further terrorizes them by promising a speedy sacking of anyone who fails to meet that month's target amount of sales.

Their future with the firm, but also their worth as persons, is determined solely by the dollars they rake in. If they cannot close their deals and get their customers to sign on the dotted line, they are worthless. The more this man talks, the more it becomes evident that for him people do not exist — only dollar figures do. At one point one of the salesmen asks the higher-up, "Who are you anyway?" His reply: "Who am I, pal? You see my watch — it costs more than your car. That's who I am!"

This portrait, while dramatically exaggerated, does sketch what many people in the workforce sense every day. When profits eclipse people, when bottom lines obscure the basic humanity of the people helping to achieve that bottom line, we quickly forget the basic care and love that we are to show to all people simply because they are people. Christian employers, whose very salvation has come by grace, can incarnate something of that divine grace by likewise freely according dignity and respect to those in their employ.

One corollary of this idea applies to overall management style. In his outstanding book *The Fabric of This World,* Lee Hardy has many good observations on diverse management styles and how these do or

46. From *Centesimus Annus,* ¶¶34-35, as quoted in Neuhaus, *Doing Good and Doing Well,* p. 296.

do not accord well with human worth. Hardy notes that as the "science" of management began to come into its own earlier this century, several methods were tried — methods that later proved bankrupt because of their poor treatment of persons. Early management theorists such as Frederick W. Taylor brutalized work by viewing humans as merely cogs in the larger machine; employees, Taylor thought, wanted and needed no more out of their work than a paycheck. This kind of cold, scientific view of work and persons increased production, but at a high human cost.[47]

Later theorists like Peter Drucker began to humanize the process by basing it on mutual respect. He recommended that employers bring their workers into the overall work process through seeking their input and listening to their ideas. This would give them a measure of control and so accord them respect and dignity within the larger work process.

In the end Hardy believes that one need not choose between people and profits:

> Work is a social place where we can employ our gifts in service to others. God calls us to work because he wants us to love our neighbors in a concrete way. The practical implication we draw from the Christian concept of work as calling [i]s simple and direct: jobs ought to be designed so that we can in fact apply ourselves — our whole selves — to our calling. [O]ur jobs ought to engage us as whole persons, as creatures with high-level capacities for thought, imagination, and responsible choice as well as motor abilities. Our jobs ought to be places where the whole person can respond to the call of God.[48]

Christian employers who are sensitive to the grace that holds us all will endeavor to humanize their work environments and to remember the gracious worth of all persons. They will also work to foster what Robert Roberts recently called "playful competitiveness." Roberts advises that while competition is an inescapable feature of human life (and an essential component to the economics of business), it need not, in the Christian perspective, be the sole goal. Rather, Roberts says, we need to have a sense of humor about the life of grace by recognizing

47. Lee Hardy, *The Fabric of This World* (Grand Rapids: Eerdmans, 1990), pp. 128ff.
48. Ibid., p. 174.

that when our finest efforts are over and done with, it is finally God's grace that enabled them and God's grace that covers the imperfections that still cling to them tenaciously like barnacles.

A Christian's sense of identity "isn't bound up with successes and achievements and recognition, although she takes on life's activities with gusto. Because Christ has cut her loose from the world's way of reckoning, she can take a playful attitude toward all contests. She may compete, but her competitiveness is playful."[49]

Of course, where the solvency of a company is on the line, it is pretty difficult for a manager or boss to be playful about it — it is, after all, "serious business." But where the worth of employees is involved (as well as the final worth of the employer), a sense of playfulness accompanied by a healthy sense of humor can help everyone recall grace. The success or failure of a firm, the varying gifts in various employees and their consequently varied abilities to contribute to a business, are not the facts on which a person gains (or loses) worth and the right to be loved, accepted, and affirmed as a person.[50]

The point of all this is that for Christians in the business world there are creative options available to help owners and employees remember grace. Individual Christians who run a business can remember (à la Deuteronomy) that even their finest profit margins and most fruitful fiscal years are finally a gift of God for which to give thanks. Within that context they can also recall that the value of any person is not determined solely on how much he or she can contribute to the bottom line. Rather, grace and graciousness dictate that we treat people fairly and humanly even as God has dealt thus with all of us. The above suggestions merely hint at some ways in which Christians in the capitalist world of earning rewards can still recall, and help others recall, that in the larger Christian vision of life grace is key. The more often

---

49. Robert C. Roberts, *Taking the Word to Heart* (Grand Rapids: Eerdmans, 1993), p. 169.

50. I realize, naturally, that lazy employees or those who pilfer from the corporation need to be dealt with realistically. That is, my advice here is not intended to communicate that all a Christian employer should ever do with an employee is smile and say with television's Mr. Rogers, "I love you just the way you are." However, under comparatively ordinary circumstances, Roberts's ideas on playfulness and a sense of humor ought to be given serious consideration.

we remember this even in the midst of our wheeling and dealing, the less likely we will ever approach Jesus in the manner of the Rich Young Man, for we will know that the most important things in life are in fact not earned; they are given.

But now to move out of the business realm, let us consider ways in which teachers and parents can instill into children (and thus also into themselves) a sense of God's awesome grace. I will assume that Christian teachers and parents *desire* to teach children of God's love and grace. Thus I will not go into great detail as to what message actively to teach (see Chapters One and Two for the C-Content of grace). Instead we will focus on practical ways in which we can conduct ourselves in the P-Content area so as not only to teach grace but also to back up that teaching with a life lived graciously.

Let us begin with some basic observations. Judith Allen Shelly has noted that although a child's spiritual formation begins early (many key concepts and ideas are communicated already in the first five years), a child will not be able to conceptualize grace until sometime after her elementary school years are complete.

> Most children [of elementary school age] see God as a celestial rule-giver as well as a helper and friend. They also see adults as rule-givers. A school-age child is legalistic and feels loved and secure when he or she knows firm limits are set on behavior. Although they may offer and accept forgiveness, their natural inclination is to do something to make up for detected offenses in order to restore a damaged relationship.[51]

We should not conclude from this, however, that it would be better not to worry about communicating grace until adolescence has begun and the conceptual hardware to understand it has developed. Rather, dovetailing with Snapper's earlier observations, this developmental fact should reinforce the need to be very deliberate in how we conduct ourselves as parents and teachers. This is so because while the concept of "grace" may be hard to grasp, children do not have a hard time implicitly picking up on works righteousness, sternness, rigidity

51. Judith Allen Shelly, *The Spiritual Needs of Children* (Downers Grove, IL: InterVarsity Press, 1982), p. 44.

of rules, or a sense of conditional love. In fact, if we hope to help children understand the *concept* of grace later in life, we had better make very certain they are observing good *examples* of grace in all the years leading up to that later point.

Toward that end parents and teachers need to have well-tuned theological antennae to pick up signals of anything that even remotely transmits a sense of conditional love, earned rewards, or feared punishments (especially punishments from God). Sunday school teachers, for instance, may wish to rethink the practice of rewarding only those who perform well. Granted ways need to be found to motivate students to do work in church education programs (programs notorious for their lack of accountability and hence of student motivation). But perhaps the teacher's own modeling can provide a better spur to students than a promised reward for good performers only (and, anyway, students who have a genuinely hard time memorizing verses, for instance, will consistently feel substandard if only good memorization merits acceptance and approbation. Their having difficulty could instead be a good place to demonstrate God's unconditionally gracious acceptance of all people despite their many, varied difficulties).

Perhaps teachers can themselves demonstrate a love of Scripture verses through memorizing them along with the children as well as modeling other examples of memorized verses that can help them later in life. Rather than approaching Scripture memorization as a grim, rote activity — the kind of thing that "we've just got to do but if you slog through, at least you'll get something in return" — perhaps teachers can model a deep-seated enthusiasm for God's Word. Perhaps such enthusiasm on the P-Content side will by itself communicate to students that learning the Bible is its own reward in gratitude to God for Jesus. If at some point in the course of a year the teacher desires to bring treats for the children, he or she should give them to all — to the good and faithful memorizers as well as to those who have not done so well. What better way to communicate the unconditional nature of the teacher's love and, by extension, of God's love?

Teachers and parents should also beware of any motivational scheme that induces guilt or fear as a goad to performance or desired behavior. I realize that in the song quoted earlier the "Father up above" is said to be looking down "in love," but that is not what sticks with most children who grow up singing it. It is the sense of being watched, and sternly watched at that, that coats their young souls like a filmy residue. It is the picture of God with a rolled up newspaper, disapproving of some actions, approving of others, but always, always judging and evaluating, that remains in a child's heart. Likewise parental words such as "What would Jesus think if he saw this?" or "Would you want to be in such a place when Jesus comes again?" subtly tell a child that certain actions or even locales can cause one to be "cut off" from Jesus' favor. Children may think that it is possible to make Jesus so sad or so mad that the child is in grave danger of being eternally swatted.

Although children do need to grow up with a sense of responsibility and although they do need to develop a proper sense of healthy shame (there are such things as right and wrong in life, after all), Christian parents need to find ways to communicate responsibility that are consistent with the teaching of grace. Children who were baptized as infants (one of the church's best emblems of grace is infant baptism) need to know that that event, though they cannot remember it and did nothing to make it happen, is their ongoing assurance that Jesus always loves them — even if they do something wrong. Nothing can block that baptismal love and acceptance, and children should be reminded of that often.

In fact, Marjorie Thompson once recommended that Sunday schools and parents make a point of celebrating not just birthdays, which everybody in the world does, but also baptism dates. As it stands, most children do not even know on what date they were baptized. But perhaps reminding them also of this anniversary can remind them of God's initiating love of grace and the ongoing acceptance to which it points.

As Donald Sloat points out, aside from our directly teaching children this, a parent's modeling of exactly this kind of unconditional love is the best way to make the God-connection. Sloat claims that the unconditional nature of God's grace is just "like the type of love we usually expect a mother to feel for her child, to accept and bestow favor on her child simply because of who the child is without setting up a series of hoops for the youngster to jump through before the favor is granted. The mother-child relationship in the family can build a powerful foundation for positive adult spiritual life, or it can create untold complications that are difficult to overcome."[52]

Parents need, therefore, to find ways to communicate ongoing

---

52. Sloat, *The Dangers of Growing Up in a Christian Home,* pp. 74-75.

acceptance and love to their children — most especially when the child has done something wrong. No punishment should be meted out by a parent without that same parent afterward initiating a warm and genuine reconciliation with at least as much (and preferably more) fervor as was evident when the punishment was dealt out.

Children need to know (and goodness knows that they test this) that nothing they do will ever separate them from the parent's love and acceptance. The more stable that awareness is, the better the child will later be able to learn about and understand the concept of God's grace and the relationship in which "[nothing] will be able to separate us from the love of God that is in Christ Jesus our Lord" (Rom. 8:39).

Above all, however, parents should never convey the notion that the child's acceptance by God has been threatened or made shaky by any action. Since the coming of Jesus, God's main reaction to sin has been to forgive it. It is not up to parents to turn the salvation-history clock back and make a child think that he or she must atone for his own sin or even that what God is going to do with a given sin is up for grabs. We know what God is going to do — he is going to forgive it. Sinning is a bad idea, and parents need to find creative ways to communicate this. The complexities of the grateful life discussed in the last chapter demonstrate that this is not easy even for adults to grasp. Unhappily, saying things like "Jesus is unhappy with you" is much easier than wrestling with the full complexities of grace. But it is also theologically dishonest and spiritually devastating to a child's grasp on grace. It is worth the creative effort, therefore, to find other ways to make children do the right and avoid the wrong.

Once again, as with Sunday school teachers, so with parents, modeling a deep, intense joy in the Christian way of life is perhaps the best way to make a child "catch" this holy fervor as well. A parent who regards life as a contest, a parent who appears to be constantly placating Jesus, earning rewards from God, or living in fear of failure and punishment, is unlikely to inspire the joy of the Christian life in the heart of a son or daughter. If an adult can keep straight what was discussed in Chapter Two, hopefully the child will be able to feel and even desire this joy of living for Jesus, too.

Finally, some advice for all Christian adults — parents, singles, and especially pastors. In recommending ways to make the Christian church and home safer places, Donald Sloat touches on the matter of spiritual honesty and integrity. In the past ministers who have dealt with young people (and parents in raising them) have tried to appear so wise, knowledgeable, and in control that many children have been led to feel that if they have doubts, questions, or struggles, something about their spirituality must be a few strokes above par. On the golf course of life, ministers often want to appear to be birdie golfers, with everyone else at least several strokes into the bogey column.

The result has been legions of people who feel that doubts are a sign of weak faith, questions are to be snuffed and stuffed, and struggles only indicate that they are more in the devil's hands than the Lord's. Even for those who are mostly outside the church, this impression has had some devastating effects. In an article about "Generation X" (people born since 1965), *Christianity Today* quoted from a number of twenty-something-year-olds who responded to queries about how they perceived the church and its ministers. Many responded along the lines of one young adult who said, "If you have questions, how do you talk to a minister who has no questions or who makes himself unapproachable?" Many of the people in this generation, the article went on to claim, are much more drawn to honest admissions of failure or struggle than they are to trumped up stories of success.[53]

As Donald Sloat recommends, ministers, especially in their public functions, would do well to admit and point out their solidarity with all people in the sinful state. They would also do well appropriately to reveal that all of us occasionally have struggles, doubts, and questions. People, including ministers, parents, and the young, do not become sinners when they sin, they sin because they are sinners. This may seem to be merely commonsense theology, but it is stunning how often people forget it — especially in churches with internal vice lists. Not so many years ago my own denomination made a list of "worldly activities" that included theater attendance, dancing, and gambling.

Now of course a lot of deep, serious thinking went into the creation of that list (and many others like it in other churches). But the fact is, as Sloat adroitly mentions, that after a while sin becomes defined as those activities alone. Avoid them, and you avoid sin; do them, and you sin! But this bifurcation of the church into the obedient versus the disobedient tends to ride roughshod over our common lot as sinners and hence our common dependence on the grace of God in Christ. Of course, while

53. Andres Tapia, "Reaching the First Post-Christian Generation," in *Christianity Today* 38.10 (September 12, 1994): 18-23.

many churches no longer have such lists formally, we all have informal vice lists that tend to separate de facto sinners from de facto nonsinners of a congregation. (This can become very evident when someone in a church is caught in some public sin. How grace should guide us in these situations will be the subject of the last chapter.)

Pastors and parents alike could do much for young people (and for themselves!) if they could validate a young person's experience by revealing that they, too, struggle, have occasional doubts, make mistakes, and so forth. It is OK to ask questions and endure struggles of temptation. And while it may not, strictly speaking, be OK to err, it is surely not the exception but the rule. But then, such failures are also the teachable moments for God's grace. The point is that by identifying ourselves with sinners, seekers, doubters, strugglers, and stragglers, we will help especially the young realize that we all need grace and that their behavior, their questions, and their struggles cannot place them outside the pale of that grace any more than adult struggles do.

One final note for preachers: Preach grace often and condemn works righteousness with zeal. The primary point of this chapter has been that the people who sit before the preacher for an hour on Sunday morning spend most of their time breathing the air and realizing the dreams of democratic capitalism. Preachers should realize that once parishioners walk out the narthex door and head back out into their workweek, very few of them will see or experience much to remind them of the kind of amazing grace that saves us all in Christ Jesus our Lord.

In fact, most of what they will see, hear, and do will point in precisely the opposite direction — the direction of "You can do it!", make your own way, earn-it-or-lose-it capitalism. Whatever merits democratic capitalism may have going for it economically, theologically it makes the life of grace that much harder to hold onto. Preachers would do well to recognize that, given the long odds they have to overcome, they cannot preach about grace and graciousness too often. True, the life of faith and the scope of Scripture are broad and rich, and not every sermon can be about salvation by grace. But if people miss the core of the gospel, they may eventually not have much truck with or use for the other parts, either.

So preachers should regularly mine the parables of Jesus, make them come alive for their congregations, and find ways to hook these wonderful stories of grace up to the lives of especially the young. And through it all the preacher should not be afraid to say that this gospel or good news is good for him or her, too. The preacher, as much as anyone sitting in front of him or her, needs God's grace every day — even, perhaps especially, in the midst of a society of achievers.

Conclusion

Our challenge in this chapter has been to find ways to be reminded of and so to live in God's grace even in the midst of such a system of earnings and rewards. What should be eminently clear by now, however, is that God's "economy of salvation" is vastly different from the economy of capitalism that surrounds us.

In Ephesians 3:2 Paul wrote, "Surely you have heard of the economy of God's grace that has been given to me for you" (my translation). Paul then goes on to say that in God's "grace economy" the precious commodity of grace is freely given to all — to Gentiles, to sinners, even to Paul who at the time was "a hatchet man for the Pharisees" (in Buechner's memorable phrase) trying to wipe the name of Jesus from the face of the earth. The mystery of this economy is that it manages its goods so poorly! It does not reckon merit; it simply grants grace freely, gloriously, and profusely to anyone whom God chooses. Unlike almost every other economic system we have ever heard of, God's gracious economy — the administration, distribution, and stewardship of God's salvation — is a giveaway.

I will leave it to others to ponder whether this stellar divine example has any implications for financial economies. But suffice it to say that all of us who have been saved by this grace, all of us who have become beneficiaries of God's loose-management system of grace, are obligated to live graciously in return. If we are stingy in giving away acceptance and love to others, if we subtly (or not so subtly) lead children to believe that they are earning their way into Jesus' favor (or sinning their way out of it), or if we base our evaluation of others solely on the basis of their ability to make money for us, we have got some lessons yet to learn from God's economy of grace. Paul tells the Ephesians that he has been charged with "making clear to everyone the economy of [God's] mystery" (3:9, my translation) of salvation. The rest of us are charged with no less.

MEDITATION

The Riddle of Grace

JUDGES 13–16

IN A BIBLE STORYBOOK I read as a boy there was a wonderful painting illustrating the story of Samson. In it Samson, looking something like a cross between Rambo and the Terminator, was in a lovely meadow single-handedly tearing a lion's jaw apart. There he was: strong, heroic Samson tackling nature's most ferocious beast. It is an inspiring image for a child.[1]

Samson is without a doubt one of the most colorful figures in the Bible. But in addition to being a strong, fearless, heroic figure, Samson has also been called an obstreperous lout, an irresponsible practical joker, and an oversexed buffoon. Sad to say, Samson was all of this and more. Still, an honest appraisal of Samson's life can teach us much.

In Judges 13 an angel announced to Samson's parents that the son they would have was to be a Nazirite. The book of Numbers describes a Nazirite as someone with a special vocation, namely, complete dedication to God. Further, the Nazirite's inward dedication was to be symbolized by certain outward signs: A Nazirite was not supposed to drink any alcohol, he was not supposed to go near or touch a dead body, and he was not to let his hair be cut. These outward signs pointed to his separation from the common and the profane.

But even a quick glance at Samson's life reveals that when it

---

1. The image of Samson as God's "Rambo" comes from my seminary colleague Roy Berkenbosch.

124

comes to having a sense of vocation, Samson chalks up a zero. God had set Samson aside for a special purpose. Not every Nazirite was promised enormous strength if he kept his vows, but Samson was so that he could deliver his people from the fierce and militarily superior Philistines.

But Samson repeatedly displays an appalling lack of common sense. As his story opens in Judges 14, Samson immediately goes down to Timnah — Philistine territory — and promptly lusts after the first Philistine woman he sees. So he runs home, tells Mom and Dad that he has found the right girl, and insists that they get her for him.

His parents are shocked. "Samson, can't you find a nice hometown girl? God told us to keep ourselves from marrying foreigners. How can you ask us to arrange a marriage with a Philistine girl?!" Samson stands up, looks his parents square in the eye, flexes his rippling muscles, and thunders, "GET HER! SHE IS THE RIGHT ONE FOR ME."

The main problem in Israel at this time was that no one paid any attention to the ways of God. Several times in the book of Judges one reads the line, "In those days every man did what was right in his own eyes" (RSV). That is the same Hebrew phrase Samson uses. "Get her for me *because she is right in my own eyes.*" Samson was supposed to be a judge in Israel — a special figure set apart as a model for the people. Yet he acted just like everyone else.

The next event is that famous incident with the lion. As Samson travels to visit his fiancée, a lion roars out to get him, but Samson finishes it off as if it were no more than a pet cat gone berserk. Sometime later he morbidly checks to see what the carcass looks like, discovers a hive of bees within it, and so scoops out some honey for himself and his parents.

But it is curious to note that Samson does not tell his parents what happened. He does not tell them that he killed a lion, and when he gives them some honey, he does not tell them where it came from. There was good reason for that. Samson was a Nazirite. He was not supposed to go near *any* dead bodies, let alone have lunch out of one! In other words, this, too, was a breach of Samson's vows.

Then Samson throws himself a wedding feast. The Hebrew word translated as "feast" in Judges 14:10 usually refers to a drinking party. We do not know whether Samson drank, but if he did, he breached yet another vow. But at this feast Samson engaged in a traditional party game. Whereas in our day the groom might toss the garter, in Samson's day the groom gave out a riddle. "Out of the eater something to eat, out of the strong, something sweet."

He wagered the bridal party that they could not guess the riddle, and they could not. But they did not want to lose their bet and have to cough up thirty linen robes. So these Philistine men pull Samson's fiancée aside and threaten to harm her if she does not weasel the meaning of the riddle out of Samson, which she does.

The answer to Samson's riddle was "honey from a lion's carcass." But when the time comes to give Samson the answer, these men answer with yet another riddle. "What is sweeter than honey? What is stronger than a lion?" Once he hears this, Samson realizes he has been betrayed by his own wife. The sad end to this part of the story is that Samson kills thirty men, takes their robes, and pays off his bet that way.

As Samson's story unfolds, he at times behaves erratically, killing willy-nilly out of a sense of personal vengeance. Eventually one reads of the famous story of Delilah, her trickery, and Samson's downfall at the hands of the very people he was to root out of Israel.

What are we to make of Samson? It is hard to say! At the center of the Samson story is a riddle. But actually Samson's whole life is a riddle. By the way, do you know the answer to the riddle that the Philistines gave back to Samson? It is quite clever when you see it because it not only answered Samson's original riddle but it humiliated him as well.

For what *is* sweeter than honey, what *is* stronger than a lion? Why, "love," of course. The men not only gave the answer, but they also humiliated Samson by hinting at *how* they got it — through his lover. But this riddle may also be the key to Samson's whole life. Samson's inability to control his libido was his perpetual downfall — his fatal flaw. Because the problem with Samson is that he always got his sweets from the unsweet.[2]

The irony of Samson's life is that the Philistines were the unclean, the uncircumcised folks who were his perpetual enemy. Yet Samson always found his honey among them. On his way to Philistia, Samson

2. Dr. Ray Van Leeuwen first alerted me to this facet of the Samson story.

took honey from the lion's carcass and then went on to marry his Philistine "honey." What is sweeter than honey or stronger than a lion? Love. The man who could tear lions apart, burst ropes like paper, carry city gates to the top of a mountain, this same man was powerless when tempted with a little honey, with a little sweet from the unsweet.

Yet, and here is the riddle of it all, God sticks with Samson. Somehow, some way, God gets things done through Samson. But how could such a buffoon be an agent of God? Why did God stick with Samson? How could God possibly have been active in the life of such a lout? Even at the end of his life, when Samson calls on God for strength one last time, God hears and answers him. In the long run Samson did accomplish keeping the Philistines at bay. The New Testament book of Hebrews lists Samson as one of the "heroes of faith." How can this be?

If we take Samson's story head-on, we are going to be puzzled by its inconsistencies. But perhaps part of our puzzlement comes because we have not yet seen our own faces in the mirror of this story. For in Samson we see the worst part of our own selves. For we, like Samson, often take our sweets from the unsweet. We also cannot escape the stain of scandal and of sin. But God sticks with us. God sticks with his church, even as he stuck with Israel, imperfect though the church often is. In history God stayed with his people, sending judges, kings, prophets, and finally his only begotten Son. God remained faithful until it hurt. God the Son remained faithful until it killed him, so that we might be forgiven.

In the final act of Samson's life, he threw himself again on the grace of God and begged God to remember him once more. And God did. In his forgiving grace and never ending faithfulness, God empowered Samson one last time. As the roof fell in on Samson's head, he died knowing that he was God's servant. He died in the arms of God's faithful and all-embracing grace.

This image reminds us of the thief on the cross, which in turn reminds us of ourselves. Like Samson and the thief, our sins and failures are killing us as we are "crucified between the sky of our intentions and the earth of our reality."[3] But then we look over, we see the Son of God

---

3. Fred Craddock, "Have You Ever Heard John Preach?" in *A Chorus of Witnesses,* ed. Thomas Long and Cornelius Plantinga, Jr. (Grand Rapids: Eerdmans, 1994), p. 40.

on his own cross, and we cry out, "Jesus, remember me." And he does. He knows that we can often be louts and buffoons, but he remembers us to his Father. He uses us to preach his gospel and to get his work done. That's the riddle of grace: the enigma of God's loving and working through imperfect people. What is sweeter than worldly pleasures or stronger than the power of sin? Why, the love of God, of course. Blessed are they who solve the riddle.

CHAPTER FOUR

Grace and Discipline

NATHANIEL HAWTHORNE'S *The Scarlet Letter* presents a strikingly grim account of church discipline gone bad. The basic story line is familiar even to many who have never read the novel: A young Puritan woman, Hester Prynne, becomes pregnant and is thus found out to be an adulteress. She is therefore consigned by her Puritan townsfolk to a state of perpetual shame, which is proclaimed to all by the scarlet letter "A" emblazoned upon her dress. For the rest of her days Hester walks the streets of her town in utter isolation, permanently separated from the fellowship of her friends and family, indefinitely cut off from the good graces of her community and church.

Hawthorne sets the tone for this story early. As the somber crowd of Puritans gathers outside the prison to witness the adulteress's appearance on a raised platform in the town square, there is

> a solemnity of demeanor on the part of the spectators; as befitted a people amongst whom religion and law were almost identical and in whose character both were so thoroughly interfused that the mildest and the severest acts of public discipline were alike made venerable and awful. Meagre, indeed, and cold, was the sympathy that a transgressor might look for from such bystanders at the scaffold. On the other hand, a penalty which in our days would infer a degree of mocking infamy and ridicule might then be invested with almost as stern a dignity as the punishment of death itself.
>
> [T]he point which drew all eyes and, as it were, transfigured the

129

wearer — so that both men and women, who had been familiarly acquainted with Hester Prynne, were now impressed as if they beheld her for the first time — was the Scarlet Letter so fantastically embroidered and illuminated upon her bosom. It had the effect of a spell, taking her out of the ordinary relations with humanity and enclosing her in a sphere by herself.[1]

Indeed, it is Hester's existence "in a sphere by herself" throughout the course of the novel that so impresses (and depresses) the reader. Whether or not Hester is contrite and penitent about her act of sexual sin is irrelevant to her upstanding townsfolk. Whether or not the sin itself might be forgivable, or indeed whether or not it *had been* forgiven by God, likewise never enters into the fray. For the rest of her days Hester exists like a specter — passing through the streets of her New England town, brushing past fellow citizens, and even doing work as a skilled seamstress — always as though she did not exist at all. She had become "hidden in plain sight" — a *persona non grata* to the highest (or lowest) degree.

Because Hawthorne's novel represents so extreme a case, it is understandably easy for readers to condemn the treatment Hester Prynne receives at the hands of those somber, earnest Puritans. It is also comparatively easy to be convinced that nothing similar ever happens today within our own church and religious communities. Still, the question to be faced in this chapter is whether we are sometimes guilty of actions and attitudes similar to those of the Puritans in Hawthorne's depiction. Just because we have never required a "sinner" in our churches to wear a scarlet letter on his or her bosom does not automatically indicate that our minds and hearts are free from the kinds of narrow, judgmental, ungracious attitudes so vividly on display in Hawthorne's work.

Obviously, the Puritans of *The Scarlet Letter* are wholly out of touch with the forgiving grace of God. For these Puritans a single wrong act could become the last word in a person's life, ushering him or her into a state of perpetual unforgiveness. In their eyes a sexual sin like Hester's made her so radically different from everyone else that only an enforced isolation could properly highlight her relationship (or lack

1. Nathaniel Hawthorne, *The Scarlet Letter* (New York: Signet Classics, 1959), pp. 57-58, 61.

thereof) to the rest of the community. Although the Puritans had a strong theology of sin and hence also a strong conception of the need for grace, their lofty conceptions of a pure church led to a tremendous concern for outward behavior and lawkeeping. This emphasis undercut both the true teaching of grace and the average Puritan's awareness of its ongoing operation in his or her day-to-day life. As Hawthorne's novel indicates, it was precisely a fixed way of life, as defined by their own legalistic and rigid code, and not the grace of God, that accounted for the difference between being a Christian and being a sinner. "Works," and not grace, determined a person's communal standing.

Given what has been said in the previous three chapters, this should be immediately obvious. However, the challenge that a novel like *The Scarlet Letter* lays at our feet is this: How do we respond when a fellow Christian is caught in some public sin? What does being gracious mean in such a situation? What does imitating the grace of God mean for us when a young woman in our congregation turns up pregnant, when an elder is caught in an adulterous relationship, when someone gets drunk and obnoxious in public, when someone is shown to be guilty of abuse?

And what if such a sin wounds me personally? What if this is a personal as well as a more broadly ecclesiastical affront? Indeed, as important as it is for us to consider how we respond publicly and ecclesiastically, we also need to probe deeply into our individual consciences to find out how we respond on a personal level. What thoughts pass through our heads regarding what should be done about this person? What suggestions for discipline do we share with one another over the coffee table after church? Whether or not formal church discipline procedures are set into motion in a given case, what do we personally wish to see happen?

These are not easy questions. In fact, the challenge to be gracious in imitation of God's grace is perhaps nowhere as great as when we are faced with the public sin of a fellow Christian. But if everything that has been said about grace up to this point is true, surely we must admit that the process of ecclesiastical discipline must also be infused with and driven by the grace of God. But, as in other portions of this study, so here we will notice that the presence of grace in the midst of such proceedings frequently serves as a complicating factor, not as a simplifying one.

131

For if church discipline were merely a matter of punishment for sin, if church discipline were no more than an attempt to clear out the "dead wood" of a congregation, it would perhaps be a simple matter. We would then have only to locate overt sinners, determine their relative guilt or innocence, and then proceed to expel those deemed guilty. In this case the whole matter would be little more than a perfunctory judicial affair regulated by rules that, if followed correctly, would usually insure a fair and just result.

But if church discipline is itself an offshoot of God's grace unto salvation, matters become quickly snarled. For grace disallows our taking on the role of final judge or jury. Grace, as the originator of our salvation, disallows our dividing a congregation up into "sinners" and "nonsinners," with the latter group standing in judgment over against the former. Grace as the power of forgiveness disallows our refusing to forgive the truly penitent and even complicates our dealings with those who are impenitent.

If we are saved by grace and not by works, if we are all sinners who are "in Christ" only because of God's gracious placement, the face of church discipline must look very different from the stern, sharp-featured visage of those Hawthorne Puritans. In short, church discipline is not all about justice and balancing the ledgers of crime and punishment. Rather, it is all about grace, which, as any child could tell you, is inherently unfair. For grace lets off the hook precisely those who otherwise would deserve some kind of punishment.

Thus in this chapter we will attempt first to determine the nature of church discipline itself. Why do we need to address this subject in the first place, and how does the Bible define the process? Once we have formally defined church discipline, we will then need to consider how grace can and should shape this practice. Finally, we need to do some unstinting scrutiny of our own attitudes toward discipline and toward those people who, for one reason or another, become potential candidates of it. We will do so to insure that we do not adopt the wrong attitudes of the Puritans but instead maintain the grace of God at the beginning of the process, throughout the process, and (above all) at the end of the process.

Before we begin, however, we should make a single qualifier. Our main concern in this chapter will be the attitudes we have in those cases where the person in question is truly penitent and sorry for his or her sin.

Although we will need to consider how to deal with those "high-handed" sinners who do not care about what they do and who likewise show no concern for Christ or his church, our main area of inquiry will be milder cases. As we will see, while grace needs to be present even when dealing with the impenitent, it is, ironically, when dealing with the penitent that we face our true challenge to incarnate the grace of God.

The Nature and Purpose of Discipline

Prior to the Protestant Reformation in the sixteenth century, few people had occasion to ask the question, "How do I know if *my* church is part of the *true* church of Jesus Christ?" Since from the time of the apostles there had been essentially only one church headed by the pope in Rome, questions regarding which church was the true church seldom if ever came up. Until that time, the only major split in the worldwide church had come in 1054, when the Eastern Orthodox churches and the Western Catholic churches split. After the Reformation, however, there was a speedy proliferation of various denominations. Before long, in addition to the two larger bodies of the Roman Catholic Church and the Protestant church, there existed under the Protestant umbrella groups of Lutherans, Calvinists, Zwinglians, Anabaptists, Mennonites, and a host of others, all quaking apart along various fault lines of disagreement (sometimes on very minor points).

Prior to the Reformation, therefore, if you belonged to a Western church, it was inevitably part of the one Church of Rome. It was the only church in town, and thus no one questioned whether it was part of Christ's true church or not — it had to be, there were no options. But once there developed such a wide variety of churches, questions as to which churches belonged to the larger *true* church of Christ became acute and urgent.

In an effort to provide helpful guidelines for those facing such questions, some of the confessions of faith that spun out of the Reformation era contain descriptions of what are called "the marks of the true church." These "marks" or characteristics are a kind of checklist of traits that any true, Bible-believing church must have if it is justifiably to be accepted as part of the larger true body of Christ on earth — the true Church. Most confessions (e.g., The Belgic Confession [Art. 29],

133

The Scotch Confession of Faith [Art. 18]) cited three such holy marks or traits that could distinguish the true church from the false: The true church of Christ must have pure preaching of the Word of God, proper administration of the sacraments (baptism and communion), and faithful exercise of church discipline for the admonition of sinners.

Our purpose is not to study these marks per se. However, inasmuch as church discipline was deemed important enough to warrant inclusion on this holy checklist, we ought not to approach this matter carelessly. Although in what follows I will occasionally be somewhat critical of the manner in which church discipline is sometimes conducted, I do not intend thereby to communicate that we would be better served not to engage in church discipline. Church discipline is a holy task to which the true church of Christ is called (indeed, along with preaching, it is also one of the "keys of the kingdom" entrusted by Jesus to his followers. Through preaching and discipline the "door" to the kingdom might be opened or closed, locked or unlocked).

But precisely *because* it is so weighty and vital a matter, we need to approach discipline with at least as much care as we do preaching and the sacraments. Further, we also need to work very hard to insure that the grace of God that is taught by the Word and embodied in the sacraments is likewise on display in how we perform the task of discipline. For if the exercise of discipline is not driven by a concern for grace, this third mark will tend to undercut the grace of the other two marks. If, in what follows, I appear at times critical of the way in which church discipline is frequently viewed or exercised, that is not because I have too low a view of discipline but precisely because I have a very high view of it. Surely the light of God's grace should stream from each of the three marks of the church and not merely from one or two of them.

But before we get into any specifics, we should begin by probing the genesis of church discipline. Where and why did this practice develop, and why did the Reformers believe it to be so important as to rank it next to preaching and the sacraments as a mark of the true church?

Current theories of church discipline likely have roots as far back as the Old Testament and its words to Israel regarding how to deal with sinners in her midst. The book of Leviticus is the key book for Israel in this regard. The slogan text for Leviticus is the oft-repeated line, "Be holy because I am holy, says the LORD" (cf. Lev. 11:44, 45; 19:2; 20:7, as well as the dozens of times when commands are followed simply by the words, "I am the LORD," which may be a shorthand way to refer to this slogan verse on holiness). This vocation of holy living, however, leads naturally to a certain amount of tension, since being holy does not come naturally to sinful people. God commands us to be holy, yet we are naturally sinful and thus unholy. This juxtaposition and dilemma are what lead to the overarching question Leviticus tries to answer: "How can a holy God live in the midst of an unholy people?"

If God was to dwell with his people, ways had to be found to remove the offense of the people's unholiness lest the purity of God's holiness be so threatened that God would have to pull up stakes and leave. After all, unholiness is to holiness what water is to fire — the two cannot come into sustained contact without the one ceasing to exist. If the Holy One of the universe was going to "live" in the midst of Israel (which was God's stated purpose in leading Israel out of Egypt), ways had to be found to remove the sin of the people so as to insure that God's reputation would not be sullied by the people among whom he lived.

It is within this context of holiness, then, that the words of Leviticus on communal discipline occur. The reason the people had to punish the wayward and expel the immoral was in order to insure that nothing happened within Israel that would threaten the all-important presence of God in their midst. No person had the right to live in such a way as to threaten the entire community's relationship with God. Strikingly, as opposed to more modern notions of individualism, the Israelites had (or were supposed to have) a radical sense of communal solidarity. What one did affected the whole, for good or for ill. It was the collective duty of the community, therefore, to police itself in order to insure that everyone lived as God directed.

As regards communal discipline in Old Testament Israel, therefore, the holiness of God and the holy integrity of the community were the key concerns. The holiness of the God who lived in their midst is what drove them to try to be holy themselves. Discipline within the community guarded this prerequisite holiness. Thus, throughout Leviticus one finds frequent reference to the need for "cutting off" from Israel those who were flagrant sinners.[2]

2. Much of my information on Leviticus comes from Gordon Wenham, *The Book of Leviticus* (Grand Rapids: Eerdmans, 1979).

Most Christian scholars agree that much if not all of the civic and legal legislation that can be found in places like Leviticus (and the legal regulations for Israel are very numerous and somewhat complicated) has now been abrogated or put aside for us as New Testament people. But we reach back to these various Levitical laws and practices of discipline because in many ways the basic principles that undergird these ancient practices have carried over into the New Testament and into contemporary theories of church discipline.

In many places the New Testament writers make clear that holiness is to be as much a concern for the church as it was for ancient Israel. Consider Paul's words in Ephesians 5:1-3, "Be imitators of God, there-fore, as dearly loved children and live a life of love, just as Christ loved us and gave himself up for us as a fragrant offering and sacrifice to God. But among you there must not be even a hint of sexual immorality, or of any kind of impurity, or of greed, because these are improper for God's holy people." Peter speaks even more directly to this idea, going so far as to quote the slogan verse of Leviticus, "But just as he who called you is holy, so be holy in all you do; for it is written: 'Be holy, because I am holy'" (1 Pet. 1:15).

In ancient Israel the honor of God and the integrity of the com-munity were the key considerations, and now these very ideas apply equally to the church of Jesus Christ. Thus today many manuals of church order and church government reflect such biblical sentiments when stating reasons for practicing church discipline.

According to the *Manual of Christian Reformed Church Government,* "The purpose of the admonition and discipline of the church is to maintain the honor of God, to restore the sinner, and to remove offense from the church of Christ."[3] Indeed, while various regulations and prac-tices have changed over the course of God's history with his people, this basic concern for the holiness of the community and for the maintenance of God's honor has remained paramount. The church is to be the body of Christ on earth. What many people think about God is going to depend on what they see in and think of God's church. Christians have an obligation, therefore, properly and carefully to re-present God to the

3. William P. Brink and Richard R. De Ridder, *Manual of Christian Re-formed Church Government* (Grand Rapids: Board of Publications of the Christian Reformed Church, 1980), p. 301.

watching world and to exhibit within their very membership the holiness of Christ and his exemplary style of kingdom living.

Toward this end the New Testament also contains various passages that inform the practice of what we now call church discipline. Although church discipline is based on and informed by a number of passages, we will briefly examine two main ones in this area. The key passage to consider is the so-called locus classicus of church discipline, Matthew 18:15-19:

> "If your brother sins against you, go and show him his fault, just between the two of you. If he listens to you, you have won your brother over. But if he will not listen, take one or two others along, so that 'every matter may be established by the testimony of two or three witnesses.' If he refuses to listen to them, tell it to the church; and if he refuses to listen even to the church, treat him as you would a pagan or a tax collector.

> "I tell you the truth, whatever you bind on earth will be bound in heaven, and whatever you loose on earth will be loosed in heaven."

Although this passage seems to address personal offenses of one person against another, the four-step process sketched by Jesus has now been applied to all forms of discipline within the church and has likewise been viewed as an overall validation of the idea that certain public sins warrant a person's exclusion from the community. The last line on "binding and loosing" has also given this entire matter sufficient spiritual weight to warrant it being called "a key of the kingdom" and a mark of the true church. As we will note in more detail below, however, the true teaching of this passage within the context of Matthew's Gospel may not be as simple as we have sometimes thought.

1 Corinthians 5 is also frequently cited as warrant for the idea that Christians have a solemn obligation to watch over the community of the church. Here the apostle Paul refers to a notorious case of sexual immorality that apparently was being tolerated by the Corinthian church community. As regards the man involved in this sin, Paul states categorically that he should be put out of the fellowship and "handed over to Satan" (v. 5). Paul then goes on to state that associating with the immoral within the context of the church's fellowship can only lead to trouble within the body.

Paul is careful to state, however, that this does not mean that Christians are never to associate with such sinners within the context of the larger society. If that were the case, Christians would never have the opportunity to witness to these people. (In fact, Paul says, if we were not allowed to have contact with *any* sinners, we would have "to leave the world"!) But Paul's point is that *within the church,* within that fellowship which is supposed to be holy and Christlike, we should not regard as a brother or sister him or her who is "sexually immoral or greedy, an idolater or a slanderer, a drunkard or a swindler. With such a man do not even eat" (1 Cor. 5:11).[4]

Although other passages could be added, these two are the most frequently cited when seeking a rationale and a method for discipline within the church. The 1 Corinthians 5 passage makes clear that, as in the Old Testament community of Israel, so too the church is to have a grave concern for its holiness and for the holiness of the Christ who is the church's Bridegroom. (Indeed, inasmuch as the Holy Spirit lives within our hearts, there is a sense in which God lives in our midst in an even more intimate and radical way than he did in ancient Israel.)

Frequently Paul holds up our unity with Christ as the basis for our being careful not to sully Christ with our own sin and evil. Given that Paul's favorite way of summing up salvation is to say that we are "in Christ," this is no surprise. Those who are "in Christ" must somehow show evidence of this spiritual "location" by being Christlike. Hence, they dare not import anything into Christ's body that does not befit holiness. (Think of Paul's striking image in 1 Corinthians 6:15-16

---

4. This last reference to eating is probably not an injunction against ever dining with someone outside the church. It is minimally a reference to the Lord's Supper. Given Paul's overall distinction in this chapter between the community of the church (where fellowship with sinners is not to be tolerated) and the larger world (where contact with sinners is not only inevitable but even necessary for the sake of the gospel), it seems likely that this reference to eating means the "love feasts" of the congregation that always led into and included the sacrament of the Lord's Supper. In other words, dinners at the homes of those not yet in the community of the church are allowable and commendable, even as Jesus himself frequently dined with those deemed "sinners" by the religious establishment of his day. So Paul is not saying that Christians may never befriend or speak with non-Christians. See Gordon Fee, *The First Epistle to the Corinthians* (Grand Rapids: Eerdmans, 1987), p. 226.

that to engage in sexual relations with a prostitute is to make the prostitute one flesh with Christ inasmuch as our very bodies are now temples of Christ.)

In summary, then, church discipline of wayward members is part of a tradition of communal discipline that reaches far back into sacred history. As in ancient Israel, so today the purpose of such discipline is to guard the reputation and holiness of God, to protect the integrity of the community in whose midst God dwells, and to deal with the sinner in such a way that he or she may cease the wrong action or pattern of activity and so enhance the community's holiness by his or her renewed way of life.

The Grace of Discipline

On the surface, discipline seems to be an activity with very little grace involved. Certainly Old Testament laws on capital punishment proffered very little hope for restoration or renewal through forgiveness! But inasmuch as the once-for-all severity of those laws has now been set aside, the question we need to face is how grace is or should be active within New Testament patterns of communal discipline and admonition. Perhaps the best way to bring the grace of God into this discussion is to return to the two New Testament passages quoted above to discover where, even in these verses, we are reminded to be gracious even as God has been gracious to us in Jesus Christ.

If, as is too often the case, Matthew 18:15-19 is read in a biblical vacuum, it is easy to miss seeing how or where grace might be operative in the four-step process Jesus presents. If we isolate Matthew 18:15-19 and so codify it into a simple matter of procedure, indeed there appear to be only two simple options: Either the person repents or he does not. If he repents, then life can go on almost as before; if he does not, then he is out — he is to be treated like "a pagan or a tax collector."

However, if we are rightly to understand these five verses from Matthew, then we must consider them not only within the scope of the entire gospel but more importantly within its immediate context. The verses on discipline within the body are "bracketed" by two parables that, while not eliminating the need for discipline, certainly qualify the way in which it is to be approached and exercised. Immediately prior to Jesus' words on the wayward brother is the Parable of the Lost Sheep (Matt. 18:10-14). Immediately following 18:15-19 comes the Parable of the Unmerciful Servant (Matt. 18:21-35). In other words, the passage on dealing with the wayward is framed by two parables that speak of the need to continually seek the lost as well as the need to forgive even the greatest of sins against us in imitation of the God who has completely forgiven us by his grace.

If the Gospels were merely patchwork arrangements of Jesus' sermons, parables, and miracles that had been sewn together willy-nilly, the presence of these two parables would not necessarily have much bearing on the meaning of Jesus' words in Matthew 18:15-19. But the fact is that Matthew and the other three Gospel writers were careful crafters, editors, and shapers of the raw gospel material. As important as the individual events, parables, and sayings of Jesus' life are, the order in which they have been placed by the Gospel writers is also intended to teach alert readers the meaning of not only the parts of Jesus' ministry but also of the whole. For this reason thoughtful Bible readers must always pay attention to immediate contexts in order to avoid misinterpreting any given incident or saying. Biblical texts such as Matthew 18:15-19 do not exist all by themselves. They are part of a larger story and of a greater teaching.

Viewed this way, it could fairly be alleged that the presence of these two parables before and after Christ's words on "discipline" is designed by Matthew to teach us that even this process of confrontation and admonition is meant to be fueled by the grace of the gospel message. If continual seeking of the lost and ongoing forgiving even as we have been forgiven are key facets to Jesus' teaching, we must see even Matthew 18:15-19 in this same grace-filled light of seeking and forgiving.

What might this mean specifically for our interpretation of this passage? It means that, even in the throes of church discipline, even when we are forced to the extreme of cutting someone off by treating him like "a pagan or a tax collector," we are not done with the need to seek and to forgive. After all, whenever Jesus ran across "pagans and tax collectors," what was his reaction? Did he not embrace them, preach the gospel to them, and forgive them by his grace?

Commentators have frequently noted the oddity that Jesus would use "pagans and tax collectors" in a negative sense in this passage given his gracious treatment of them everywhere else. Some commentators feel that Jesus was merely using the pejorative terminology of his time to communicate his point. That is, Jesus knew that most Jews shunned "pagans and tax collectors" and would have nothing to do with such "low life." So in this passage he used those words in their most pejorative sense to drive home the point that a total cutoff was sometimes needed for the sake of the church's holy integrity. So, some allege, what Jesus was essentially saying was, "A person who will not repent after repeated confrontation is as bad and undesirable as those miserable pagans and tax collectors. Avoid them like the plague!"

But there is something amiss in that interpretation. Certainly one cannot deny that Jesus is communicating something negative by referring to these two groups of people. However, given Jesus' endemic abhorrence of the way pagans and tax collectors were treated in his day, it is highly unlikely that he would ever step outside of his ordinary mindset and so deliberately play into popular (mis)understandings of how those people stood in relationship to God's kingdom. Suppose a white preacher from the 1960s spent much of his time preaching racial harmony and equality to the mostly white congregations of his city. Can you imagine such a preacher ever saying, "If you run across someone who won't repent, treat him like a nigger!"? Such an utterance would be so out of character for a preacher committed to racial harmony that he could never say such a thing without thereby undercutting and vitiating his main message of equality and love. So also with Jesus. He would never aid or abet wrong and pernicious conceptions of the very groups he came to love.

It is more likely, therefore, that while Jesus was communicating a sense of "outsideness" by referring to "pagans and tax collectors," if his words are read within the larger context of his ministry (as well as in the immediate context of the parables preceding and following this passage), one would have to say this: If someone remains recalcitrant in a certain sin or sinful lifestyle, you are to regard him as outside the community of faith.

However, those outside the community, even those considered as far outside as pagans and tax collectors, are precisely the proper target for loving gospel proclamation. Pagans and tax collectors are among those "sick people" whom Jesus came to heal. They were the ones among whom Jesus spent most of his time and among whom he did his best ministry. So, yes, if someone sins, we may for a time have to regard him as being outside the community. But we do not for that reason cease having contact with him. We are to continue seeking these "lost sheep" and, if we find them, we are to continue to hold out the offer of the same gracious forgiveness that we ourselves have experienced at the hand of God. No debt is so great that it cannot be forgiven, as Jesus himself subsequently teaches in the Parable of the Unmerciful Servant. "Pagans and tax collectors" may have been outside the community of the faithful in Jesus' day — but it was for that very reason that Jesus worked so hard to bring them inside through preaching the offer of his holy grace.

Yet another key gospel teaching that we dare not forget when approaching the matter of discipline, and that is also highlighted by the two parables in Matthew 18, is that when we approach someone who is wayward, we are to do so not as a superior judge but as a fellow sinner. We, too, were once lost sheep who were dependent upon the gracious determination of the Good Shepherd in order to be found. We, too, once owed the unpayable debt of the servant in the story and so were dependent upon the grace of the King through Christ to release us from that debt.

The community of Christ was forged by the unstinting grace of God in Jesus Christ. If, in the heat of church discipline, we forget this and so become uncompassionate, unduly harsh, judgmental, or simply unforgiving, we show how little we know ourselves and how seldom the reality of grace forgiving our own sin registers in our hearts. The Parable of the Unmerciful Servant immediately follows Jesus' words on the wayward as a reminder that "it is by grace we have been saved, not by works," and that if we refuse others that same grace, we shipwreck the gospel on the shoals of our own self-righteous zeal.

Thus, although the holiness of God and the integrity of the community require that we be willing, ready, and able to confront one another on lifestyles inimical to the gospel, we must do even this in a way true to the gospel of grace. Even in those comparatively rare cases when we must go so far as to treat someone "as a pagan or a tax collector," the need to seek out and to proffer forgiveness goes on and on.

In fact, despite Paul's sharp words in 1 Corinthians 5 about the man caught in sexual immorality, although such a person could not be regarded as a brother within the community, once he was out of the community, he, too, would become the target for loving, graceful evangelism. Indeed, in another case the Corinthians did just this with another such person in their midst.

2 Corinthians 2:5-11 speaks about the need to restore to the fellowship a certain sinner who had responded in godly grief to the

admonition and discipline of the church. Although in the past some have conjectured that this is the same person as the man in 1 Corinthians 5, most now doubt this. Still, as commentator Gordon Fee points out, the restoration of this person shows the pattern Paul would like to see followed for all who offend. The person in 2 Corinthians had also been guilty of a terrible sin — one that caused Paul much personal grief. But as soon as Paul got word of this person's repentance, Paul changed his tone immediately (as befitted one who knew of God's grace for the heinous sins he himself had committed) and so urged the Christians in Corinth "to reaffirm your love for him" (2 Cor. 2:8).[5]

So even in the most extreme cases — cases that, to use contemporary terminology, go all the way to excommunication — the need to be loving, gracious, and proffer gracious forgiveness never ends. While the holiness of God and the integrity of the body of Christ might necessitate separating ourselves from those whose lives do not in any way reflect Christ, we dare never cease showing concern for the sinner, seeking the lost, and offering forgiveness to even the worst offenders. If "pagans and tax collectors" were Jesus' chief target of ministry and hence the chief recipients of his grace, if Paul could so quickly reaffirm his love for someone whose sin had pained him so deeply, the church of Jesus Christ dare never forget to minister to and be loving toward even those whom she has painfully needed to cut off.

Earlier, however, we noted that our chief concern in this chapter would not be the hard-core cases that actually go so far as censure and excommunication, but rather more typical cases of people who are caught in some sin but who also show remorse and repentance. Since these cases come up with greater frequency than those of the unrepentant ones, we need to spend some time pondering how grace should affect our thinking in these areas.[6]

To do so it would perhaps be helpful to examine such situations

---

5. Ibid., pp. 213ff.

6. Indeed, most denominations have recorded a fairly sharp decline in actual excommunications, censures, and the like. This may be due to a loosening up of discipline in general, but it likely also owes to the greater fluidity of our society and the ease with which people now change churches or simply resign from them. Whatever the causes, the fact is that actual cases of formal discipline no longer come up as frequently as do the kinds of cases to be considered below.

by way of a case study approach. The example that follows is fictional, although in my effort to target a fairly typical situation some might be led to believe that I am writing about a specific, given case. That is not my design, however. Rather, what follows will be a kind of conflation or telescoping together of various similar situations I have experienced as a pastor as well things I observed during the years when I was growing up in the church.

Suppose that in a fairly tight-knit congregation a single woman, April Jones, becomes pregnant. Suppose further that April has taught for many years in the church's Sunday school program and has also at times been active in the congregation's Girls' Club. In short, April is not simply a member of the church but is also a visible, high-profile member of the church community. But now she has become pregnant and, having deemed the possibility of abortion unchristian, will soon carry the result of her sin in a most obvious way.

Suppose lastly that, upon learning of her pregnancy, April goes to her pastor and elder to confess, with great remorse and obvious contrition, the error of her ways. In addition, she relates the sexual struggles she and her boyfriend have had but also states that, having talked about it, they had decided that a quick marriage could only compound their problems; indeed, it remained to be seen whether they would ever wed. Still, in the midst of her earnest and tearful confession, she begs the church's forgiveness — even going so far as to indicate a willingness to acknowledge this sin publicly in whatever forum the consistory deemed appropriate.

The question that faces any pastor or group of elders who has ever confronted such a case is this: What does one do next? Should April be told that it would be best if she resigned her teaching post in Sunday school? Should she be placed under some form of censure, thereby at least temporarily preventing her from partaking the Lord's Supper? Should any kind of formal church discipline be set into motion? And what should be done once the child is born, if April decides to keep it? Especially if she and her boyfriend have yet to resolve the question of marriage, should the child be baptized as a covenant youth of the congregation?[7]

7. I am obviously writing out of my own tradition, which includes infant baptism.

Before answering all these questions, let us take note of some of the reactions that frequently arise within the hearts of other members of the congregation upon learning of this "public" sin. In my experience there are always a few who immediately urge the pastor or elders "to do something about this." The sentiment is that within the church of Christ we cannot tolerate sin lest it appear that we also condone it. A person such as April should surely *not* be allowed to continue in worship, the sacraments, and certainly teaching Sunday school as though all were well and as though such actions did not carry some weighty church discipline-like consequences.

Many if not most members would certainly urge that she be removed from any publicly visible role such as Girls' Club or Sunday school, and not a few would be quite pleased if she were simply "put away," removed from sight altogether. Certainly, especially in the absence of marriage, a baptism ought not to take place. In fact, I once heard someone suggest that any time someone in a congregation had an illegitimate child whom she kept, the child should be baptized "in private" (perhaps at someone's home). In this way the other children and young people of the congregation would not see this spectacle and so be led to think that this was an acceptable way to have children! "After all, the church must not be soft on sin."

It is precisely here that we must stop and try very hard to remember grace. It is precisely when thoughts such as, "We've got to *do* something about this . . ." begin to occur to us that we must remember that while the holiness of God and the integrity of the community must be preserved, neither of those all-important things are helped along if the church rides roughshod over the grace of God. For a major part of God's holiness is his grace. The source of the church's integrity is likewise grace.

While there may be times in the life of a congregation when the only way to preserve the integrity of the church is to cut off one of its wayward members, far more often the holiness of God and the integrity of the church can best be shown forth in that the church of Christ is first and last a place of grace. There is no better way to highlight this holy fact than by forgiving the penitent and embracing those sheep who have stumbled or temporarily lost their way. As we noted in Chapter Three, very few facets of our society remind one of grace. Many organizations, clubs, firms, and businesses will not give a wayward member or employee a second chance. The church of Christ must be the one place where grace abounds, giving not only second chances, but third, fourth, fifth, and "seventy times seven" chances.

When church members sin, but when they likewise show remorse and a desire to be forgiven, it is the obligation of the church to imitate the grace of Jesus and simply forgive them. Period. The goal of church discipline is to bring about godly grief and penitence. When that is already present, no further, formal steps are to be taken. We may want to counsel with this person. We may want to find ways to encourage him or her not to repeat this sin. We may want to do other acts of loving, gracious compassion to insure that he or she feels secure within the community as well as that in the future he or she will be able to contribute to the community's wholeness and holiness.

But to suggest that "something should be done about her," when her remorse is already present, is to turn church discipline into a tool of punishment. Discipline of any kind is first and last a tool of grace — the grace taught in the gospel and incarnated by the sacraments. When discipline departs from the grace of the Word and sacraments, these other two marks of the true church also suffer damage. Remember: The job of all believers in the church is not so much to forgive as to *recognize* the forgiveness already granted by God in Christ and then to imitate that on both an ecclesiastical and personal level.

When a person seeks forgiveness in true penitence, the church does not have to *do* anything about him or her — everything has already been done by Jesus, the Christ of God. If we want to see the punishment of this person's sin, we need look no further than the cross. The cross is God's punishment for all sins — public and private. We minimize the significance of Jesus' sacrifice if we feel that we must come up with individual punishments to supplement the punishment already endured by Jesus on the cross.[8]

To suggest that he or she should be put "under discipline" demon-

8. I recognize, as Lewis Smedes has often noted, that while forgiving may come comparatively easily to God (and it was no cinch for him, either), it often comes with even greater slowness for us. Depending on the circumstances, forgiveness may be a desperately hard thing for individuals as well as for churches to accomplish fully. But the point here is that when remorse is present, the task of forgiveness, and not the task of discipline, is what we must begin working on.

strates that we have forgotten that all of us come to church every week as remorseful sinners. Only the impenitent should be placed under formal discipline in the hope of fomenting penitence and thus opening him or her to the marvelous power of God's grace. In the meantime, each person lives in the power of grace and so has an obligation to be gracious in the face of the sins and failures of others. If we begin to think that only those engaged in publicly obvious sins need grace, we enter into the error of the self-righteous discussed in Chapter Two. As soon as matters of discipline become a kind of "us versus them, sinners versus non-sinners" scenario, we have lost grace. As soon as we begin to think that we have to "do something" about the penitent sinners in our midst, we have forgotten about our own need for grace and thus violate that very grace.

Remembering Grace

But if the church cannot in this world ever be free from the stain of sin and scandal, and if at times we truly must engage in formal church discipline procedures, how can we keep the grace of God before us when encountering such situations? Assuming that we do not want to forget and thus violate God's grace at those junctures when someone's sin visibly enters the church, how can we remember and so enflesh grace especially at such times? What follows is a list of practical tips or suggestions of ways in which we might better be able to deal graciously with those who have fallen into some kind of public scandal. Once again, the main focus here will be on those less extreme cases in which the person is genuinely penitent (although much of what is said below could also apply even to those cases that actually necessitate more formal proceedings).

The first thing to keep in mind is our common solidarity in sin and thus our common need for God's grace. This may seem so obvious that it scarcely warrants mention. However, the simple fact is that when someone like April turns up with some publicly obvious sin, many people quickly begin to think in terms of "us and them." Suddenly those of us who have not so sinned begin pondering what we should do about those who have. Suddenly we think that his or her public sin is so serious that we forget that each of us comes to church each week with a slate full of sins equally in need of God's grace unto forgiveness.

Of course, while all sins are bad, some sins are more grave than others — not in the sense of needing more grace in order to be forgiven but in the sense of doing more damage to the church's reputation and integrity in a public way. While all sins are bad in God's sight, some sins do more harm. So, for instance, Jesus made clear that lusting in one's heart is as culpable in God's sight as actually waking up in the wrong bed one morning. But few would judge the fantasy to be as harmful as the actual adultery. Whereas both sins need grace to be forgiven, only the actual adultery could even potentially warrant discipline-like concerns. In other words, there is warrant to distinguishing between different levels of sin, with some being more appropriately of corporate concern than others. Indeed, the entire prospect of church discipline forces us to make such distinctions.

Even those outside the church recognize something like this type of distinction. Think of President Jimmy Carter's infamous interview with *Playboy* magazine in which he confessed to having occasionally lusted in his heart. For those outside the church such a confession seemed merely quaint. After all, such a fantasy could not possibly qualify as a sin, could it? Carter, earnest Christian that he is, knew better. At the same time, however, if Carter had admitted having had an actual adulterous affair, the public uproar from both Christians and non-Christians would have been as terrific as the one caused in 1992 when rumors of Bill Clinton's possible infidelity surfaced. (Or think of how Gary Hart's presidential campaign derailed in 1988 after revelations of his various trysts.) The point is that most people distinguish between various levels of sin, with some sins having clearer public ramifications than others. Carter was right to recognize both fantasy and adultery as being sins that are culpable and thus in need of grace unto forgiveness. Carter's home church was likewise right, however, in not placing him under discipline for admitting fantasies within his heart.

The problem we face in remembering grace in such matters, however, is not in making the appropriate distinction between public and private sins. The difficulty arises when we begin to think that *only* publicly visible sins are real sins and that, as long as one is not caught, or as long as the fantasy remains in the heart, it is really not so bad at all. To think this way is to buy into popular but wrongheaded notions of what sin is. As Neal Plantinga has pointed out, most people today conceive of sin as something merely episodic. That is, "sin" is not something with which you are born or of which you are guilty in general; rather, you become a "sinner" if you do something wrong (and are caught doing it). But the Christian view has always reversed the order: We do not become sinners when we sin; we sin because we are born sinners. All of us, irrespective of whether we commit a sin about which everyone knows, are equally in need of God's grace.

In fact, one irony of the New Testament is that sexual sins, while bad, are often presented as no worse than sins such as greed, pride, gossip, envy, and gluttony. In many ways these "spiritual" sins are *more* pernicious and dangerous for Christians than are more public sins. The reason for this is that sexual sins, for instance, are likely to be caught and thus addressed whereas smoldering anger or deep-seated pride might continue for years without ever being challenged.

A man who once committed adultery will probably be passed by when nominations for elder are presented. But a man who for years has been an envious gossiper and backbiter could probably be elected over and over. A pastor seen coming out of a pornographic movie theater can anticipate swift trouble. A pastor who is regularly seen gorging and glutting himself at area "All You Can Eat" buffets, however, is less likely to be censored. Yet as C. S. Lewis once put it, a self-righteous prig is probably a lot closer to hell than is a prostitute — although it is better to be neither. But we would do well to reflect on the fact that most of the "Seven Deadly Sins" are sins of the heart and thus not likely candidates for discipline. For that very reason, however, they are the more dangerous and need just as much grace and personal discipline as do those sins that flicker in the public eye. All of us are sinners, and some of us have much deeper problems than do those who come under public scrutiny.

Remembering this fact is what kindles compassion when faced with a pregnant single woman, a struggling homosexual, or some other congregational member for whom a particular sin has become more widely known. Recalling our own incessant need for grace, recalling the enormous debt that has been paid off by Another on our behalf, inclines us to be gracious toward and forgiving of others. Some sins may be more publicly serious and damaging than others, but no one can claim exemption from sin such that he or she has the right to judge another sinner gracelessly or to withhold gracious forgiveness from him or her.

When it comes to setting oneself up as judge over another penitent sinner, all Christians should, to use a legal term, "recuse themselves." When judges recuse themselves, they refuse to hear certain cases because their personal biases would perhaps keep them from being fair, from delivering truly "blind" justice. So in the church: When someone is penitent and seeks the same grace we need every day, we dare not pass judgment or claim that such grace is withheld by God and thus should be withheld by the church. We must recuse ourselves because we are not fit to hear this case. We know too much about ourselves to be entrusted with so weighty a judgment. Anyway, this case has already been heard by Another, and we must accept that he has already declared innocence.

One way to keep this sense of our own sin constantly before us *within a church setting* (which, as it relates to discipline, is precisely where we need to remember this) is to take very seriously our weekly confession of sin as part of the Sunday liturgy. (Here I am assuming that we have not given in to the ways of those trendy churches that have dumped the confession of sin because it is not "seeker sensitive.")

In Chapter Two we discussed the need to remember our own sin on a daily basis as a way to keep us from becoming conceited in our own virtues. Doing this in an ecclesiastical setting as we sit in the congregation of our brothers and sisters is also necessary to remind us that the church is a gathering of the graced, not a collection of the morally superior. But too often our weekly public confession of sin is a merely routine and perfunctory action that the average worshiper does not take seriously. But if we hope to keep our perspectives straight and clear, we must realize that, every week, that particular time in the worship service is our time to confess our very real sins.

Yet we forget this. In a striking passage of *The Scarlet Letter,* the town's minister, the Rev. Mr. Dimmesdale (who, unknown to the townsfolk, is the father of Hester Prynne's illegitimate child), is tormented by his own guilt and the hypocrisy with which he has carried on as the church's pastor while Hester has borne the brunt of the town's scorn and shame. At one point in his personal torment he fantasizes how wonderful it would be to unburden himself by publicly confessing to his congregation that he, too, is a miserable, rotten, low-down sinner. He reflects on how good it would feel to have that out in the open rather than let people go on believing that he was sinless and without fault. But then he realizes, to his horror, that even if he *did* publicly confess his sense of guilt, it would do no good.

More than once, Mr. Dimmesdale had gone into the pulpit, with a purpose never to come down its steps until he should have spoken words [of confession]. More than once, he had cleared his throat and drawn in the long, deep, and tremulous breath, which, when sent forth again, would come burdened with the black secret of his soul. More than once — nay, more than a hundred times — he had actually spoken! Spoken! But how? He had told his hearers that he was altogether vile, a viler companion of the vilest, the worst of sinners, an abomination, a thing of unimaginable iniquity; and that the only wonder was that they did not see his wretched body shrivelled up before their eyes by the burning wrath of the Almighty! Could there be plainer speech than this? Would not the people start up in their seats by a simultaneous impulse and tear him down out of the pulpit which he defiled? Not so, indeed! They heard it all, and did but reverence him the more.[9]

Why did they reverence and esteem their minister even after he had hundreds of times spoken words of self-loathing and confessed his vile sinfulness? Because these were, after all, liturgical words. Pious people were supposed to acknowledge their sin and vileness before God, but no one took that seriously. That was just "church talk." Had they known that their minister had been Hester's lover, they would indeed have torn him from the pulpit and emblazoned an "A" on *his* chest. In other words, there was plenty of grace for abstract sin but apparently none for concrete, actual sin.

Everyone knew the doctrine that they were all sinners, and everyone went through the weekly liturgical motions of confessing that sin before the Almighty. But let someone's sin become real and visible and obvious, and suddenly the people did not know what to do, except for excising him or her from the community of those whose sin was "safe," that is, not real. As Roger Lundin recently wrote, "The result is that in the world of Hawthorne's fiction, a sinner has only two options — pretension or banishment. Without the possibility of forgiveness, self-conscious sinners must either conceal their guilt or endure their ruin."[10]

We are, unhappily, not so very different from those Puritans. We

9. Hawthorne, *The Scarlet Letter*, p. 140.

10. Roger Lundin, *Culture of Interpretation* (Grand Rapids: Eerdmans, 1994), p. 157.

know all about our sin in the abstract, but all too often those generic, nameless sins fail to generate compassion when we are faced with the public, nameable sin of someone else. Somehow we must find a way to remind ourselves that the only sins that are forgiven are actual sins. Sins in the abstract do not need forgiveness because there are no such things. So while public sins are more damaging than private ones, we dare not forget that all sin needs grace and that the actual sin of each one of us places all of us in the same boat. To forget grace, to refuse to give grace, to refuse to accept someone's repentance for even the most public of sins is to show how little we know ourselves. Worse, it shows how little we know our Savior.

We need, therefore, a healthy awareness of our own sin. Remembering that sin and seriously confessing it by name in church each week may be one way we can avoid the trap of thinking that the church contains no sinners except when a public scandal erupts. We should not need a public scandal to remind us of the fact that the church is full of sinners in need of grace. If we can take our own sin seriously on a weekly, daily basis, and then use that as a goad daily and weekly to celebrate the amazing grace of God in Christ, we will be the better poised to deal lovingly with any in our midst who fall seriously and so find themselves in need of some serious grace-giving and forgiving.

Second, in addition to remembering our own personal sin and hence our ongoing personal need for grace, when scandals erupt we must also find ways to deal with such matters with our children. The person who suggested that illegitimate children be baptized "in private" and so out of the public eye of the congregation was showing a horribly judgmental attitude. She was also showing a wholesale misapprehension of the nature of the sacraments as public ceremonies for the whole church. Baptism initiates one into the covenant community by the washing away of sins through Jesus' blood.

To suggest that this could be done in the absence of the community, to suggest that some members of the congregation should be sneaked in through the back door so that the sin involved would not unsettle the rest of the church is as ludicrous as it is graceless! The simple fact is that even the most upstanding parents who present a child for baptism do so as forgiven sinners — sinners who are as dependent on those waters of baptism for cleansing as is the little one they are bringing to the font (which is the point just made above —

when we are in church, we must remember that we are in an assembly of people each of whom has a problem with sin). To suggest that a baptism be done in private in order to keep people from seeing sin within the sacrament is like suggesting a dirty car be washed at night so that the neighbors will not realize that your car had gotten dirty! Baptism is a sacrament of cleansing precisely because we all need a wash. There is no way to keep sin out of it. (If there were, we would not need baptism in the first place!)

But let us leave that to one side and assume that this person expressed a wish for a private baptism out of a legitimate concern for those children and young people who would witness the spectacle of a single woman presenting for baptism a child born out of wedlock. Would this, as this person feared, tell children that we in the church condone sin or think that having a baby in this way was acceptable or normal? Not at all — or at least not necessarily, provided parents did a good job of using such an occasion not to indulge their penchant for graceless judgmentalism but rather as a "teachable moment" for grace.

In Chapter Three I asserted that one way to help children grow into grace is for parents to admit their own weaknesses and limitations and so demonstrate, in ways subtle and obvious, that parents, too, need Jesus' grace and forgiveness. I also mentioned that pastors would do well to admit the struggles of life rather than pretend that all is well with themselves and so foment guilt in the lives of those who are earnestly struggling with sin. Although no pastor would want to turn the baptism of an illegitimate child into a kind of tawdry sermon illustration (to the embarrassment of all), parents surely could use such an occasion privately to celebrate grace with their children.

Children could be told that, no, what she did was not within the boundaries of God's intention for sexuality. No, it is not right to have sexual relations outside of marriage and, yes, doing so can lead to many problems and considerable personal pain (that is *why* God tells us not to do this — it is always a good idea to communicate to children that God's laws are not arbitrary but really are designed to make life as enjoyable as God originally intended). At the same time, however, the baptism of such a child could be turned into another opportunity to say to children, "But, just as we've always told you, even when we make mistakes and sin, Jesus loves us anyway. Miss Jones made a mistake, but that doesn't mean Jesus stopped loving her. He has forgiven her and loves her little child, too. That's why the minister baptized him this morning — to show that God loves us even when we're bad, even when we mess up. He wants us always to live for him, but he knows we make bad mistakes sometimes, so that's why he died on the cross."

Make no mistake: A baptism of this kind would require careful instruction on the part of parents. Children, especially those who are old enough to be aware of what is going on, would likely ask some hard questions about why Miss Jones would have done this and what it all means. In short, it creates some awkwardness, and that is probably why the person mentioned earlier tried to avoid all that by having the baptism occur outside the public eye. But sin, all sin, *is* awkward. We cannot avoid its awkwardness by pretending that actual, public sins never happen.

But parents who have done a good job teaching their children about grace will doubtless find it much easier to deal with such a situation than will parents who have subtly taught their children that God loves us only when we are good. Parents and pastors who have freely acknowledged and taught that we all need the grace of Jesus, and that nothing we ever do can cut us off from that grace, will discover in such a baptism not the condoning of sin but the shining effulgence of grace.

Lastly, in order to be realistic, we need to ponder another kind of issue. I have already asserted that where genuine repentance is present, formal church discipline procedures need not be initiated. As John Calvin pointed out, since the restoration of the sinner through a goading toward repentance is the goal of discipline, discipline should be stopped as soon as such repentance is in evidence — the goal would have been achieved.[11] However, what if, as in our fictional case study, the person in question is a Sunday school teacher? More acutely, what if the person involved in a scandal is a pastor? Should they automatically be released from those positions? Should a pastor be expected to leave a congregation? Would even a temporary suspension from office be unduly harsh for a pastor caught in some public sin?

These are difficult questions and, in some ways, they should only be dealt with realistically and pastorally on a case-by-case basis. Hard-

---

11. John Calvin, *Institutes of the Christian Religion,* ed. John T. McNeill, trans. Ford Lewis Battles (Philadelphia: Westminster Press, 1960), IV.12.8, 1236.

and-fast pronouncements designed to be "one size fits all" kinds of advice ought not to be made. Still, a few general words about grace's impact on even these issues can be spoken.

In terms of the Sunday school teacher, there is no generally clear reason why the woman in our scenario would automatically have to resign or be removed from this position. If the congregation is steeped in the teaching of God's grace, and if parents do a good job of teaching their children that this woman's sin, while indeed a sin, is forgiven by God even as our own sins are, I can see no theological reason why she would have to leave the Sunday school.

Realistically, however, remaining in such a position might be difficult — especially during the obvious stages of pregnancy. The simple fact is that some parents will not understand what grace is all about. Nor will some parents teach their children about grace but instead become furious over the thought of their children sitting in front of an obviously pregnant single woman. Such people will kick up enough dust that for her to remain as a teacher will likely bring this woman more grief than good. It is perhaps at a time like this that Paul's "weaker brother" arguments from Romans 14–15 would come into play and hence, for the good of the community, she would perhaps at least temporarily have to leave her post after all.

But such an action would indeed be a grudging concession to the "weaker" members of the congregation — to those who struggle with understanding grace. Such a removal could be avoided, and one of my main points in addressing the grace of discipline is that it should be avoided. When it cannot be, however, some will immediately and smugly see her stepping aside as a kind of punishment for her sin. Some members may even think that such a punishment is only appropriate. They might cloak this by insisting simply that "actions have consequences," and we cannot pretend otherwise. "When a high-profile person commits a public sin, he or she cannot expect that there will not be repercussions." But if a pastor or elder senses that some members of the congregation want a form of punitive action taken against a fellow member, these people themselves need to be admonished!

No form of church discipline is designed to be punitive. Yes, sinful actions have consequences, and if a Christian desires to find out what kind of consequences, he or she should reread the passion accounts in the Gospels. The cross is the consequence of our sin. God will not punish us further for it, and neither should the church take it upon itself to punish any of its members.

Practical realities and the offense caused in "weaker" members may necessitate a Sunday school teacher's resignation in the light of a public scandal. But if this is perceived in any way to be doling out punishment, if this is done in such a way as to be a kind of public slap on the wrist, once again we have lost grace and have set ourselves up as judge over the already forgiven. Shame on any Christian who thinks that it is his or her job to punish those whom God has already forgiven! Sinful actions may hurt us as a consequence of the deeds we have done. But that is a different kind of consequence than viewing church discipline as a kind of direct punishment *for* the sin.

The same is true in the case of a wayward pastor. Admittedly, no situation in the church is as potentially damaging or as deeply painful as when a respected pastor is caught in a grave public scandal. Much spiritual trust can be violated and tremendous damage can accrue to a pastor's reputation when this happens, and no amount of previous preaching about grace on his part will completely ameliorate or wipe out this pain and this damage.

Here, too, there is no theological reason why such a pastor, if properly penitent, could not be restored even as the apostle Peter was reinstated after his threefold denial of Jesus. Practically, however, it may be very difficult if not impossible for a pastor to resume work in the same congregation where the public scandal erupted. Even congregations who have done an outstanding job of being gracious to a fallen pastor would have a very difficult time reinstating him or her as though nothing had happened.

Again, theologically this could be done. Realistically it is not so easy. Of course, minor scandals could be overcome such that a pastor could continue to serve in the same place. But the larger the scandal, the greater the amount of trust that will have been eroded. Still, if such a pastor is penitent, is willing to undergo a time of suspension to pull himself or herself together and receive serious spiritual counsel and guidance, there is no reason to suppose that such a pastor could not continue to serve somewhere else.[12]

---

12. Of course, sometimes cases arise that involve a long-term pattern of abusing the pastoral office such that there might be legitimate reasons to wonder

All too often, however, church councils feel that it is their duty to punish a pastor, and a removal from office, even a temporary one, is frequently viewed less as a step along the road to restoration and more as a kind of slap in the face. But an awareness of grace requires that where genuine repentance is in evidence, accompanied by a wholesale willingness to reform through the Spirit's help, there compassion, gentleness, and mildness must be in evidence. As Calvin stated, "This gentleness is required . . . that it should deal mildly with the lapsed and should not punish with extreme rigor, but rather, according to Paul's injunction, confirm its love toward them."[13]

Remember: The most infamous case of pastoral failure was Peter's denial of Jesus. But the Gospels are very clear that Jesus' response to this failure of his most devoted follower (the "rock" upon whom Jesus would build his church) was grace from first to last. Mark 16:7 sums up the entire gospel in just two words when the angel tells the women on Easter morning, "But go, tell his disciples *and Peter,* 'He is going ahead of you into Galilee. There you will see him'" (emphasis mine). Likewise John 21:15-19 should bring tears to the eyes of anyone who has ever failed his or her Lord but who then felt the shining power of

---

whether this person should or could ever continue in that office in *any* place. Again, my words in this regard are general and can only be guideposts along the way for specific cases, which perforce must be dealt with on an individual basis. Some also feel that there is a difference between dealing with a pastor's professional status versus dealing with his spiritual status, such that we might regard him as fully restored and forgiven spiritually even if we defrock him professionally. Again, there may be cases where it is deemed that a given person ought not to be entrusted again with the pastoral office. However, once again the church of Christ can best *be* the church when it deals graciously even with a pastor's professional status. Just because lawyers who break the law are disbarred and doctors who malpractice lose their license does not mean that pastors who fall must automatically be defrocked. While there is some warrant to distinguishing between the pastor as person and the pastor as professional (and while most church orders distinguish between general discipline for all members and special discipline for office bearers), we should not pretend that grace is active only in general discipline but not necessarily in special discipline. Perhaps a given pastor does need to be defrocked because of gross professional abuse. But even this must be done carefully, thoughtfully, and, above all, graciously.

13. John Calvin, *Institutes,* IV.12.9, 1237.

grace warming the soul again. For there the risen Lord Jesus comes face to face with Peter for the first time since the denial and, in three quick steps, restores Peter fully and completely, "Feed my lambs; take care of my sheep; feed my sheep." While practical realities might make matters more complex for us when dealing with pastors in scandal, the overall tone of our dealings with such penitent pastors ought never to be more than a heartbeat away from Jesus' gracious dealings with his wayward disciple.

Summary

Discipline within the church of Jesus Christ aims to maintain the honor of God, preserve the unity and integrity of the church, and call sinners back to repentance. All three of those vital tasks are best accomplished when the grace of God is in the driver's seat. For a major part of God's holiness is his grace. The fountainhead of the church's integrity is God's grace. The way for any sinner to repent is by the impulsion of God's grace. Grace is what creates the very things we wish to maintain and defend. Grace must, therefore, also be the way by which we maintain and defend them.

The presence of proper discipline and admonition has long been regarded as a way to distinguish the true church from the false. But if there is one thing this book has tried to make abundantly clear, it is this: The true church of Jesus Christ is a living example of God's grace unto salvation. If any church fails to communicate the wonders of that free grace in its preaching, in its observance of the sacraments, or even in its exercise of discipline, that would perhaps be as sure an evidence as any that this church must itself be something of a false church. For there is no gospel other than the gospel of grace, and there is no salvation other than that made available "by grace alone through faith alone." Anyone who tries to be saved (or even tries to stay saved) through any other means is living untrue to the gospel of Christ. And as Paul once wrote to the Galatians, "But even if we or an angel from heaven should preach a gospel other than the one we preached to you, let him be eternally condemned!" (Gal. 1:8).

For the vision of the gospel is finally the vision of grace. It is within the scope of this vision that the church must locate herself. Of course, we all err and wander away from a pure apprehension of the gospel. We all find it easier to be judgmental than forgiving, stern than gracious. Like the unmerciful servant in Jesus' parable, all of us occasionally revel in God's forgiving us our enormous debt only to turn around and nail someone for his or her own more trivial debt. Amazingly, grace is available even to forgive us for our times of gracelessness!

That this is so, however, is no excuse not to incarnate God's grace in the words we speak and the lives we lead. For it was, after all, our sin that made the intervention of God's grace necessary. It should come as no surprise, therefore, that the sins of our brothers and sisters present us with our finest opportunity to be gracious. For if we cannot be gracious when dealing with someone's actual sin, when do we think we ever will have opportunity to be gracious? What do we think the grace of God is *for?*

Conclusion

LEWIS SMEDES has written that the experience of God's grace is like the experience of another world. "A first experience of grace could feel as if we have landed in a world where 2 + 2 might knock at our door and introduce herself as 5, where when a wrench falls out of our hand, it rises to the ceiling. There is a weightlessness about grace. It has the feel of a fairy tale; what makes it a very special fairy tale is that it is true."[1]

If there is one point I hope this book has made clear, it is that grace is indeed "otherworldly." The world of God's grace does not work like the world in which we mostly live. That is why I have contended that, while grace is the greatest news ever, while grace is a comfort and joy beyond words, *living* that grace in a gracious life creates all kinds of complex dilemmas and perspective-challenging choices. For we are involved in a kind of "war of the worlds" as God's grace seeks to overturn most of this world's ways of reckoning merit, earning goods, or settling scores. Even as 2 + 2 = 5 would seem ridiculous to our conceptions of arithmetic, so the giveaway of grace, when applied to the situations we have covered in this book, will at times appear to be unfair if not simply unworkable.

But, as we have also emphasized, there is tremendous power in God's grace. Grace may have to swim upstream as it battles this world's

---

1. Lewis B. Smedes, *Shame and Grace* (San Francisco: Harper and Row, 1993), p. 110.

currents of legalism, antinomianism, and capitalism, but it contains more than sufficient strength to do so. Our task as Christians is not to resist this powerful force but to allow it to shape and, where necessary, recast our ordinary ways of thinking and being.

In his famous sermon "You Are Accepted," the theologian Paul Tillich said, "It would be better to refuse God and the Christ and the Bible than to accept them without grace. For if we accept without grace, we do so in a state of separation [from God] and can only succeed in deepening the separation."[2] Only the grace of God can bridge the chasm that sin blasted out between the Creator and his creatures. Only grace can usher us into the world of God's salvation. And only grace can transform our lives while we are still in this world so that our citizenship in God's "world of grace" can be evident to all. To live gracious lives in this ungracious world requires that we overcome long odds. But, by the very grace that saves, we have good hope of achieving this.

For there is finally a kind of cosmic "fittingness" to the graced also being gracious. Indeed, as the last stanza of "Amazing Grace" makes clear, we will never finish graciously saying "Thank You" to God for his grace:

> When we've been there ten thousand years,
> Bright shining as the sun,
> We've no less days to sing God's praise,
> Than when we'd first begun!

That is the world of grace toward which we are traveling and of which we are already citizens. Being gracious is our vocation as members of that world; it is our part in the cosmic dance of Creator with creation, Redeemer with redeemed. For the dance of grace will be the dance enjoyed by all at the eternal wedding reception that follows the heavenly marriage of the Lamb to the church. The Bride of Christ must, already in this life, do all she can every day to practice her gracious footwork and learn the necessary steps so that when that grand and glorious wedding day dawns, she will be ready to take the Groom's lead and "trip the cosmic light fantastic" — the light of glory, the light of grace. Let the dance begin.

2. Paul Tillich, "You Are Accepted," in *A Chorus of Witnesses,* ed. Thomas Long and Cornelius Plantinga, Jr. (Grand Rapids: Eerdmans, 1994), p. 99.

Index

Antinomianism, 49-50, 53, 70
Augustine, 29

Bailey, Kenneth E., 39n.17
Berger, Peter, 87
Boice, James Montmomery, 20
Buechner, Frederick, 24, 28, 81, 82, 112

Calvin, John, 11, 58-59, 90-91, 154, 157
Capitalism: and children, 106-9; definition, 94-97; and grace, 7, 92, 98, 100, 108-9, 114-17, 123; and Reformation, 90-91; and theology, 98-100, 105-6
Capon, Robert Farrar, 6, 11, 38, 48-50, 52-53, 59, 66, 67, 69, 86
Carter, Jimmy, 102-3, 148
Children, 7, 25, 106-9, 117-20, 145, 152-54

DeVos, Richard, 89-90, 95-97, 105, 113
De Vries, Peter, 64-65, 66n.11
Dyrness, William, 101, 102, 104-5

Ecclesiastical discipline: and grace, 7-8, 133, 142, 147, 150, 153-55, 158-59; history of, 133-39; nature of, 132, 143, 146-47, 155, 158-59; in Scripture, 134-39

Faith, 28-29
Forgiveness, 58, 140, 142, 146, 148, 151-53

Grace: business and, 113-17; and capitalism, 7, 92, 98, 100, 108-9, 114-17, 123; children and, 7, 25, 106-9, 117-20, 145, 152-54; definition, 4, 13-14; and discipline, 7-8, 133, 142, 147, 150, 153-55, 158-59; faith, 28-29; favor, 16-17, 21-22; and graciousness, 4-5, 13-14, 58-59, 60, 69; and gratitude, 6, 59-60, 63-65, 73, 76-77; Gospels, 6, 12, 30-41; and law, 12, 14, 23-26, 31-37
Gratitude, 6, 59-60, 63-65, 73, 76-77
Guinness, Os, 92-94

Hardy, Lee, 114-15

163